EXPLORE THE WORLD

TENERIFE

Authors:
Heiner Schwarz,
Michael Reimer,
Wolfgang Taschner

Up-to-date travel guide

NELLES

Dear Reader: Being up-to-date is the main goal of the Nelles series. Our correspondents help keep us abreast of the latest developments in the travel scene, while our cartographers see to it that maps are also kept completely current. However, as the travel world is constantly changing, we cannot guarantee that all the information contained in our books is always valid. Should you come across a discrepancy, please contact us at: Nelles Verlag, Schleissheimer Str. 371 b, 80935 Munich, Germany, tel. +49-89-3571940, fax. +49-89-35719430, e-mail: Nelles.Verlag@t-online.de

Note: Distances and measurements, including temperatures, used in this guide are metric. For conversion information, please see the *Guidelines* section of this book.

LEGEND

★★ ★★	Main Attraction *(on map)* *(in text)*	Santa Cruz *(Town)* Iglesia *(Sight)*	Places Highlighted in Yellow Appear in Text		Expressway
★ ★	Worth Seeing *(on map)* *(in text)*		International/National Airport		Principal Highway
❽	Orientation Number in Text and on Map		Nature Reserve		Main Road
	Public or Significant Building	Teide (3717)	Mountain (altitude in meters)		Provincial Road
	Hotel	\ 13 /	Distance in Kilometers		Secondary Road
	Shopping Center		Beach		Pedestrian Zone
✝	Church		Ancient Site		Car Ferry
	View Point		Cave	$$$	Luxury Hotel Category
			Tourist Information	$$	Moderate Hotel Category
				$	Budget Hotel Category *(for price information see "Accomodation" in Guidelines section)*

TENERIFE

First Edition 2000
ISBN 3-88618-728-4 (Nelles Travel Pack)
ISBN 3-88618-783-7 (Nelles Pocket)
Printed in Slovenia

Publisher: Günter Nelles
Managing Editor: Berthold Schwarz
English Edition Editor: Chase Stewart
Photo Editor: K. Bärmann-Thümmel
Cartography: Nelles Verlag GmbH
Lithos: Priegnitz, Munich
Printed By: Gorenjski Tisk

- S02 -

TABLE OF CONTENTS

LIST OF MAPS

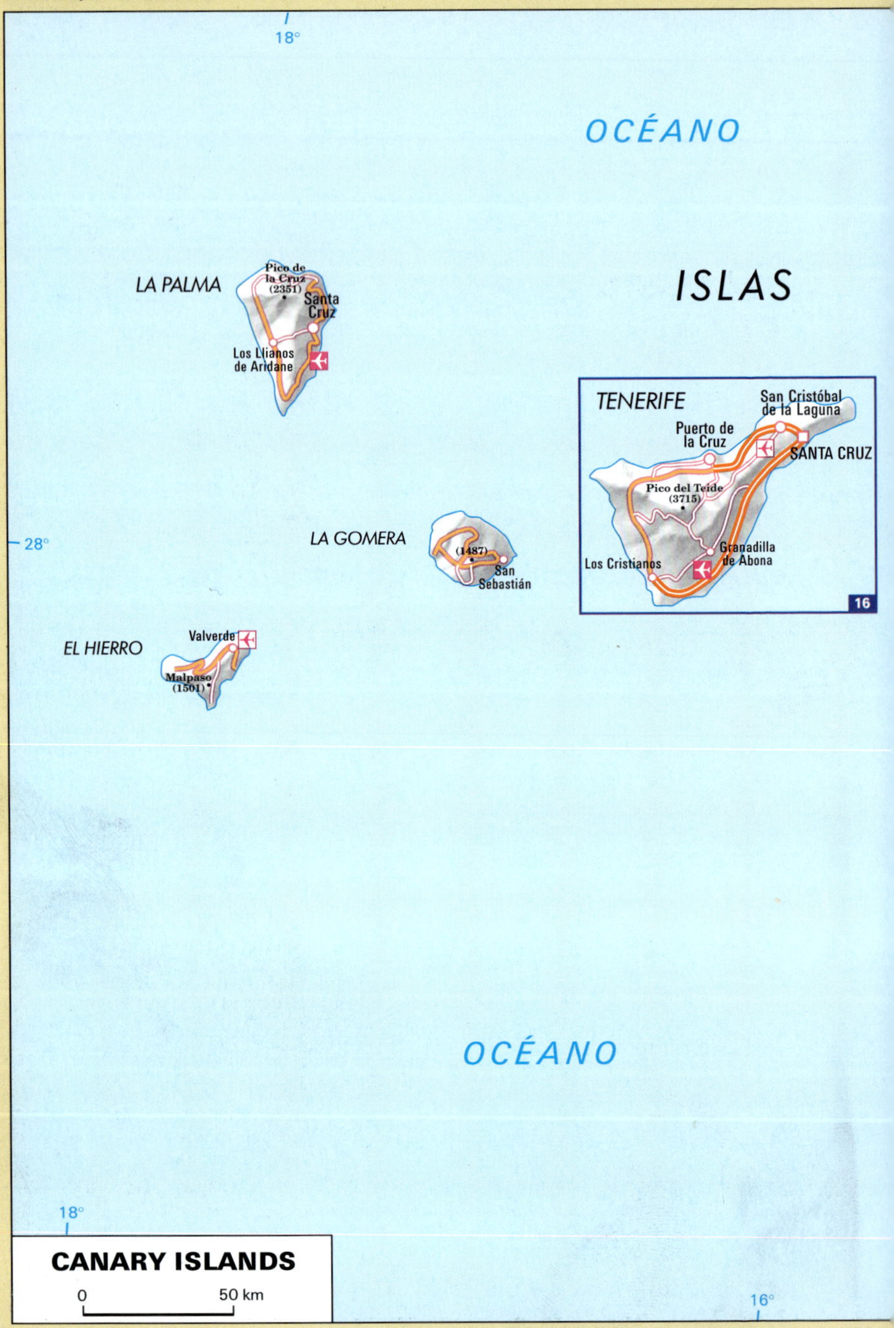
18°
OCÉANO
ISLAS
LA PALMA
Pico de la Cruz (2351)
Santa Cruz
Los Llianos de Aridane
TENERIFE
San Cristóbal de la Laguna
Puerto de la Cruz
SANTA CRUZ
Pico del Teide (3715)
Granadilla de Abona
Los Cristianos
16
28°
LA GOMERA
(1487)
San Sebastián
EL HIERRO
Valverde
Malpaso (1501)
OCÉANO
18°
CANARY ISLANDS
0
50 km
16°

14°
ATLÁNTICO
ALEGRANZA
MONTAÑA CLARA
GRACIOSA
LANZAROTE
CANARIAS
(SPAIN)
(608)
Arrecife
Playa Blanca
Corralejo
LOS LOBOS
FUERTEVENTURA
Puerto del Rosario
Betancuria (724)
Gáldar
LAS PALMAS
Gran Tarajal
Jandía (807)
Pico de las Nieves (1949)
28°
Moro del Jable
GRAN CANARIA
Maspalomas
Laayoune
ATLÁNTICO
MAROC
Lemsid
14°

Prehistory and Antiquity

2500-1000 B.C. Early tribes from the Mediterranean area settle on the island, presumably including the *Gabel-guanxeris.* This is where the name of the aboriginal population, known as the Guanches, is derived from.

800 B.C. The ancient Greek writers Homer and Hesiod praise what they refer to as the "happy islands" out in the Atlantic beyond the Strait of Gibraltar

25 B.C. In an attempt to explore the Canary Islands, the Romans send King Juba II of Mauretania out on an unsuccessful expedition.

Middle Ages

6th-9th centuries Berber tribes from North Africa make their way to the eastern Canary Islands.

14th century Under the guise of doing trade, the Spaniards, Portuguese and Genoeses dock on the coast of Tenerife. They rob and enslave the natives instead, giving rise to a bloody insurrection that is responded to with punitive expeditions.

1342 Pope Clement VI not only claims the diocese of El Teide for himself, but also demands an annual tribute of 400 guilders from the Canaries.

1492 During an excursion, Columbus observes a volcanic eruption of Mount Teide and stops on the isle of La Gomera in order to stock up on provisions. Some weeks later he will start from here on his voyage to America.

1494 One year after defeating La Palma, the Spanish conquistador Alfonso Fernández de Lugo tries his luck once again on Tenerife, however, the fierce resistance of the Guanches leads to his defeat in the Battle of Mantanza.

Under the Spanish Crown

1495 After two failed military campaigns, Alfonso de Lugo finally overcomes the native resistance at La Victoria on Christmas Day, and Tenerife is conquered, as the last of the Canary Islands, by the Spanish crown after more than a century of military conflicts.

16th century There is a flourishing slave trade on all isles of the archipelago, despite the objection of the Catholic Monarchs of Castile. The slaves have to work on sugar-cane plantations and in vineyards; Malvasía wine is exported.

1647 Encouraged by the large profits of sugar-cane cultivation, the British admiral Robert Blake tries to occupy Santa Cruz in an assault with 36 ships, however, like his fellow countryman Admiral Jennings, some 50 years later, he fails. Pirate raids are increasingly becoming a nuisance, bringing trade to a standstill more than once.

1797 During the attack on Santa Cruz, Admiral Nelson suffers the only loss of his career. Later he utterly destroys the Spanish navy during the famous Battle of Trafalgar.

The Guanche Museum in Orotava offers a glimpse into the life of the original Canarians.

1799 Alexander von Humboldt stops over on his journey to South America to study the island. He climbs the Pico del Teide and is fascinated by the diversity of the volcanic landscape.

19th century The vines that have guaranteed a steady source of income for so long suddenly become diseased. Although the loss is temporarily compensated for by the production of red dye from the cochineal insect, the introduction of aniline dyes quickly puts an end to that dream. The resulting poverty compels many inhabitants to emigrate, mainly to Venezuela and Cuba.

1817 The first university of the archipelago is inaugurated in La Laguna.

1852 To stimulate the economy, Queen Isabella II declares the Canary Islands a free-trade zone.

1872 Wine production finally ceases and the export of bananas gains in importance.

1880 In Puerto de la Cruz tourism starts; 10 years later the Gran Hotel Taoro is built. The British introduce bananas as a monoculture.

Nowadays, the EU supports the production of the aromatic dwarf banana on Tenerife.

20th Century

1912 With the introduction of *cabildos insulares* (island councils), each isle of the archipelago is granted a kind of self-administrative body.

1927 A decree is introduced that divides the Canary Islands into provinces. The province of Santa Cruz de Tenerife comprises the western islands of Tenerife, La Palma, La Gomera and El Hierro.

1936 The new Spanish republic votes a leftist alliance into the government for the first time. This startles General Franco, who has been staying on Tenerife, to such an extent that he mobilizes his followers to prepare a military putsch, initiating the three-year-long Spanish Civil War. His victory leads to a dictatorship lasting until his death in 1975.

1957 In Puerto de la Cruz tourism is on the increase. The first charter flights arrive on the island. The sun-seeking passengers are accomodated in the 12 existing hotels.

1960-70 Tourism advances to become the foremost source of income. Despite a capacity of 23,000 beds for visitors, Santa Cruz surrenders supremacy to Playa de Las Américas in the south, where a building boom has started.

1975 After Franco's death, Juan Carlos I is named King of Spain. The Moroccans march into the Spanish colony of Western Sahara.

1977 One of the worst accidents in aviation history, in which 577 people are killed, takes place at Tenerife's Los Rodeos Airport. Soon thereafter, the Reina Sofía Airport, a model of safety, is opened.

1978 An organization known as Pro African Unity compels Tenerife to stop fishing along the Saharan coast unless the Canary Islands agree to declare themselves part of Africa. This suggestion, needless to say, does not meet with the approval of the population. On December 7, Spain finally receives a democratic constitution, raising Spanish hopes and expectations.

1982 The Canaries are declared an autonomous province.

1986 Spain becomes a member of NATO and of the European Union. Special status is negotiated for the Canary Islands, which is to remain in effect until 1996. Cigarettes and alcohol are, up to a certain limit, now as before subject to a customs exemption; a sales tax of 4.5 percent applies in place of Value Added Tax.

1992 The EU approves the "Poseicon" scheme, which guarantees the provision of vital resources to the Canaries on the basis of special measures.

1996 While the special status of the Canaries within the EU is partially abolished making way for full integration, the number of tourists on Tenerife exceeds the magic four-million mark.

1998 Owing to the Schengen Agreement there is no longer passport control for those traveling from EU-member countries.

TENERIFE
A Continent in itself

THE SUNNY SOUTHWEST
THE NORTHWESTERN TIP
THE OROTAVA VALLEY
THE NORTHEAST AND ANAGA
SANTA CRUZ / LA LAGUNA
THE ARID SOUTH
LAS CAÑADAS AND TEIDE

"Isle of Hell" with Ten Climatic Zones

Tenerife towers above all the rest. The summit of Mount Teide, covered with snow or sulfur depending on the time of year, can be seen from far and wide. The highest mountain in Spain braves the trade winds, absorbing life-giving moisture from the clouds that crowd around its peak. Gran Canaria has been referred to as a "continent in miniature," but this applies more to Tenerife. There are up to 10 climatic zones on the "Isle of Hell," as Tenerife was known to medieval writers; four differently-shaped mountain ranges make up the relief, extensive forests turn into deserts of boulders and scree reminiscent of moonscapes, and there are broad sand beaches here too.

Tenerife has become so popular that formerly unspoiled and beautiful regions – such as the Orotava Valley that was praised so highly by Alexander von Humboldt – have now been turned into large built-up areas. Formerly barren coastal strips have been transformed into large vacation centers. Tenerife is the largest of the Canary Islands, and has a good traffic infrastructure – so finding your way around and exploring in a rental car is a good idea. Luckily, though, there are regions that can still only be properly explored by hikers, and for many they make up the real Tenerife.

Like most of the Canary Islands, Tenerife has two sides to its climate: there's the one sheltered from the wind, where it's almost always summer, and the one towards the wind where climatic conditions are rather more spring-like. The south is warm and dry, and the north is pleasantly moderate – but also cloudy and damp, especially in the winter months. Hikers therefore prefer the north and the center, while beach fans head south. Water sports and paragliding can be indulged in all over the island.

Previous Pages: Investigating the endemic flora of Tenerife. Snow-capped Mount Teide, the "Mount Fuji of the Canaries." View from the Anaga Mountains of the offshore Islas de Fuera. Left: The carnival in Santa Cruz provides strong competition for Rio de Janeiro.

Arrival

The main port of entry to the island for vacationers is the international **Aeropuerto Reina Sofía** in the south. There are car rental firms here, public buses and taxis; you can exchange money at the bank, and the tourist information office can provide information on accommodation and sights. If you're arriving by plane from the other islands, you'll usually land

Map pp. 16-17, Info pp. 53-59

OCÉANO
ATLÁNTICO
Playa de los Barcos
Punta del Fraile
Buenavista
Los Silos
ROQUE DE GARACHIO
Garachico
El Tanque
Playa de San Marcos
San Marcos
Icod de los Vinos
San Juan de la Rambla
Icod el Alto
La Guancha
Playa Martiánez
Puerto de la Cruz
Los Realejos
Tigaiga
Faro de Teno
Punta de Teno
Teno Alto
MACIZO DE TENO
El Palmar
Tierra del Trigo
Mirador
San Juan del Reparo
Cuevas Negras
Los Erjos
Puerto de Erjos (1100)
Masca
Bco. de Masca
Santiago del Teide
Finca de Guergues
Casas de Araza
Playa de Bco. Seco
Tamaimo
Arguayo
El Volcán Negro (1626)
Mña. de Abeque (1745)
Pico del Teide (3717)
Pico Viejo (3135)
Mña. Blanca (2750)
VALLE DE
Bco. Hondo
Mña. del Al de Guamas
El Portillo
(2148)
Centro de Visitantes
Parque National del Teide
LAS CAÑADAS
Acantilados de los Gigantes
Los Gigantes
Puerto de Santiago
Playa de la Arena
Bco. de Guía
Mña. del Cedro (2265)
Mña. Cangaro (2195)
Roque de García
Guajara (2717)
El Sombrero (2534)
Paisaje Lunar
Alcalá
Guía de Isora
Playa de San Juan
Taucho
Bco. del Infierno
Vilaflor
Las Calderas (1371)
Roque de los Brezos (1111)
Granadilla de Abona
VALLE DE SAN LORENZO
Callao Salvaje
Adeje
Roque del Conde (1003)
Arona
Valle de San Lorenzo
San Miguel
La Caleta
Playa de Las Américas
Mirador de la Centinela
Playa Las Vistas
Los Cristianos
Aero-puerto Reina Sofía
El Mé
Los Abrigos
Roja (171)
Costa del Silencio
Punta Ro
El Palm-Mar
Las Galletas
Punta Callao
Faro de Rasca
Playa de San Blas
Playa de la Tejita
Gomera, La Palma
TENERIFE
0 5 10 km

Roque de Dentro
Roque de Eurea
Las Palmas
Faro de Anaga
Roque Bermejo
Chamorga
Roque de las Bodegas
Punta del Hidalgo
Punta del Hidalgo
Chinobre (910)
Taganana
Bajamar
Chinamada
Las Carboneras
El Bailadero
Punta de Anaga
Taborno 1024 m.
Mirador Rico del Inglés
Las Montañas de Anaga
Tejina
Punta de Antequera
Valle de Guerra
Las Mercedes
Mirador Cruz del Carmen
Tegueste
Playa de los Gaviotas
Cádiz
El Pris
Las Canteras
San Andrés
Punta de los Órganos
Mesa del Mar
La Laguna
Playa de las Teresitas
Tacoronte
Aeropuerto Los Rodeos
El Sauzal
Gran Canaria
Santa Cruz de Tenerife
La Esperanza
La Matanza del Acentejo
La Victoria del Acentejo
Rincón
Santa Úrsula
Mirador Humboldt
Bosque de la Esperanza
La Orotava
Orotava
Aguamansa
Los Órganos
Candelaria
Arafo
Mña. el Limon (2108)
Mña. de la Crucita (2040)
Playa de Samarines
Güímar
Izaña
Mña. de las Vacas (2363)
Valle de Güímar
Mirador de Don Martin
Bco. de Herques
Playa de Arriba o las Bajas
Fasnia
Playa de los Roques
Arico
Punta de los Requetés
Sanatorio de Abona
Bco. del Río
Punta del Sordo
Océano Atlántico
Playa del Tambor
Playa de Médano

at **Los Rodeos** airport, near La Laguna in the north. There, too, you'll find car rental firms, buses and taxis. The ferries from Cádiz and Gran Canaria arrive at the capital Santa Cruz de Tenerife, while the ones from Gomera and La Palma dock at the harbor of Los Cristianos. Here, too, there are plenty of taxis and buses around.

THE SUNNY SOUTHWEST

El Médano

If you're crazy about surfing wind and waves, then **El Médano** ❶, located east of the international airport, will be like paradise. It consists of modern buildings grouped around a small sand beach and a broad plaza beyond it, which is used for fiestas and which becomes the social center after siesta time. On the western side is a small beach promenade with ice-cream parlors, cafés and restaurants. There are more restaurants on the eastern side of the plaza and also down at the fishing harbor, where the narrow streets make everything more atmospheric. The main attraction here, however, is definitely windsurfing. El Médano is one of the 10 top addresses in the world for windsurfers, and international competitions are held here every year. Accommodation, courses and equipment are all provided – and there's no better feeling than surfing across the bay with your eyes on the **Punta Roja**, a red volcanic cone at the end of it!

Above: El Médano is one of the world's top 10 windsurfing centers. Right: Golf del Sur, one of the four golf courses in the south.

If you only come here to swim, there's an endless sand beach just 10 minutes' walk away from the western side of the town: the **Playa de la Tejita** (nudity is also partially tolerated here, by the way) with its light sand that has been baked into tuff at some locations. There are no plants and no shade as far as the eye can see, and hardly any protection from the wind either. Miniature "dust devils" are a common sight here. A little farther west, **Los Abrigos** ❷ has made a name for it-

self as a provider of seafood specialties. The rocky bay here, which forms a natural harbor, is lined with an astonishing number of fish restaurants, all with views of the sea. On nice weekends they're usually packed, especially the *Perlas del Mar*, which is magnificently located up on a rock on the eastern side of the harbor. If you're lucky, freshly-caught fish may just be arriving down at the harbor – and it will arrive on your plate very shortly afterwards, garnished beautifully and utterly delicious.

To reach the next coastal village to the west you first have to turn inland. After a golf course, the green grass of which contrasts markedly with the dark earth colors of the desert-like landscape here, you'll arrive at **Costa del Silencio**, a chessboard-like conglomeration of hotels and apartment blocks, with a few stores and restaurants of its own. The town of **Las Galletas** ❸, which replaced the former fishing huts here, is also full of new buildings. Behind a narrow, dark pebble beach there's a pedestrian promenade with ice-cream parlors, cafés and restaurants that is actually the only place people can walk here. The name of the apartment village, *Ten-Bel* (short for "Tenerife-Belgium"), makes it clear that a lot of Belgians spend their vacations here.

An enormous, brightly-painted quay wall encloses the bay of Las Galletas. Anyone looking for a bit of a change can watch the fishermen landing their catches here, or stroll past the anchored yachts. The protected harbor is ideal for windsurfing beginners who find the waves at El Médano too difficult to negotiate – you can wobble around on your board a lot more easily here without having to fall in all the time!

Incidentally, if you feel like exploring the underwater world of this volcanic island massif, try visiting the diving schools at Costa del Silencio and in Las Galletas, which also provide useful lessons for beginners. Golfers and golf hopefuls will find a golf school near the turnoff to El Palm-Mar, with a nine-hole course.

Los Cristianos and Las Américas – The Tourist Centers

In early photographs, **Los Cristianos** ❹ looks like a sleepy little fishing village at the end of the world. The fishermen are still here, but no one is sleepy any more, least of all the tourists returning from the all-night discos. Los Cristianos now takes up an entire inhospitable stretch of barren coastline, and its apartment buildings, hotels, restaurants and stores extend high up the surrounding slopes. In the town center, the modern **Plaza del Carmen** is the center of social life for the inhabitants as well, so Los Cristianos doesn't appear half as sterile as many similar towns. The light sand beach is protected by the large harbor wall and is very popular with families. Fishing boats, ferries and excursion ships coming and going also ensure that there's always something to see.

Above: The daily bustle on the kilometers-long beach promenade of Playa de Las Américas. Right: Surfing in wintertime.

The newly laid out sand beach to the west of the center, the **Playa Las Vistas**, is larger and a lot more cosmopolitan. Its pedestrian promenade leads as far as the northern end of the **Playa de Las Américas** ❺, the town's far busier rival when it comes to filling beds and pampering streams of visitors.

While Los Cristianos still has an old-fashioned, relaxed edge to it, Las Américas is action 24 hours a day. Not a lot of sleeping goes on around here. The pubs and discos are often open at any time of the day or night, ready to cater to the wishes of excitement-hungry guests. The most notorious center of all this action is **Las Verónicas**, with its continuous thumping music. There were several battles here in the past between very violent and mainly British youths and the island police, who at first were not equipped to deal with them.

You usually have to look twice to realize that life in Las Américas, which has several beaches protected by breakwaters, is not that bad after all. Plenty of wa-

ter from the mountains ensures that the plant life here thrives, and many a tedious-looking modern building has been esthetically rescued as a result. Some of the hotels are miniature botanical gardens in their own right. Hotel buildings in every modern style also constitute the main sights of Las Américas. One very striking establishment is the exclusive *Bahia del Duque*, with its blend of super-modern and Canarian traditional architecture.

Playa de Las Américas caters to every spare-time activity you can think of, and a lot more besides: there are swimming pools and tennis courts at virtually every hotel here, and entertainers and "animators" work tirelessly to keep the guests fit and merry. Water parks, sailing, diving, paragliding – everything marketable or merely "in" can be found here.

The tourist boom in Las Américas also resulted in the construction of numerous modern buildings in **Adeje** ❻, which until the 1980s used to be an inconspicuous but picturesque small village in the hinterland. An avenue lined with laurels passes through the historic center, and numerous restaurants and bars have their tables outside. At the end of this main street there's a freshly-renovated little church, the two-aisled **Iglesia Santa Úrsula**. Alongside its Mexican-style belfry and a remarkable ceiling construction in the presbytery dating from the 17th century, the church also contains a special relic from the feudal era: a barred balcony above the sacristy from which the former lords of Adeje – members of the influential Genoese family of Ponte, who also owned Gomera and Hierro at some time or other – used to listen to Mass being celebrated.

The Ponte family's fortified residence dating from the 16th century, the **Casa Fuerte**, is only a ruin today. The former manor house can be found to the northwest of the church, at the start of the hiking path into the Barranco del Infierno. A cannon once used against pirates stands on a small hill nearby.

For hikers, the ***Barranco del Infierno** is a nice, easy introduction to the special qualities of the landscape on Tenerife. From Adeje, a well-surfaced path leads to an 80-meter-high waterfall, which can be very or not so wet depending on the time of year. In peak season this ravine gets quite full of people, so you can't expect it to be that peaceful (the hike there and back takes around three hours altogether).

Along the West Coast

As you continue driving along the coast road in a northwesterly direction, you'll pass banana plantations and newly claimed land, revealing that the real estate boom in the southwest of the island still hasn't peaked. Tourist enclaves such as La Caleta or Callao Salvaje will probably grow together one day.

Playa de San Juan ❼ has been around for quite a while, but its white buildings look very modern. The most interesting feature of the place is the harbor, protected by a large harbor mole, and also a dry dock. There's always something going on here: fishermen can be seen mending their nets, and boat-builders painting their ships.

A detour inland leads to **Guía de Isora**, where the almond trees blossom very beautifully every spring. The large amount of water and the fertile soil in this region have made it a center of potato and tomato cultivation. The church of **Virgen de la Luz** contains not only a renovated Artesonado ceiling, but also two Madonna statues by José Luján Pérez, the famous Baroque woodcarver from Gran Canaria.

The next village to the north of Playa de San Juan, **Alcalá**, is rather a rarity in this part of Tenerife – it's one of the very few places in the southwest not to have sold out to tourism. The village is located right next to the sea with a view of Gomera, and has a harbor inside a small bay on the steep coast. The central plaza still retains the relaxed atmosphere of the good old days, and it's definitely worth soaking up that feeling for a short while.

Right: The attractive black sand of the Playa de la Arena, with a view of Gomera.

At the end of the coast road is the former fishing harbor of **Puerto de Santiago** ❽, which has long since been transformed into a vacation resort and has grown together with its modern satellite town of Los Gigantes. The main attraction here is the well-tended, dark sand beach of **Playa de la Arena**, where wooden planks protect your feet from the scorching sand. Some fishermen still leave from here, but most of them seem to earn more taking tourists out on boat trips to the bays outside all the local barrancos and back again.

In **Los Gigantes**, large and sprawling apartment complexes can be seen all over the slopes. The quiet streets are full of luxuriant vegetation, and wind their way gracefully through this hilly town. Los Gigantes is named after the up to 600-meter-high and 10-kilometer-long ***steep coast**, which is worth a boat trip on its own. You can find a boat at **Puerto Deportivo** (yacht harbor) at the foot of the enormous rocky cliffs, where various attractive ships lie at anchor – and the voyage to the steep cliffs is definitely worthwhile. The dark beach is protected by quay walls, so children can bathe quite safely there.

While you're winding your way up around the hairpin bends to **Tamaimo** and looking down at the terraced tomato fields below, you may catch sight of a paraglider coming down from the Ladera del Bicho if the thermals are right. It's a sport which has become increasingly popular in recent years, and the conditions around here are especially suitable. Some paraglider pilots are so skilled that they can use thermals to fly upwards rather than down, and soar around for hours on end. Tamaimo is an ambitious little place that is doing its best to earn

Map pp. 16-17, Info pp. 53-59

money from the tourists by selling craft products like embroidered cloths.

Just before the plateau of Santiago del Teide there's a turnoff to **Arguayo** ❾, near which you'll find lava dating from the last eruption in 1909. Today you can still see which fields the lava covered and which ones it spared. Arguayo used to supply the entire southwest of the island with clay vessels, and traditional pottery (without the use of a wheel) has recently been revived as part of a state-financed project. In the **Centro Alfarero**, a small museum on the main street, you can see the latest generation of potters at work.

THE NORTHWESTERN TIP
Rocky and Unspoiled

Santiago del Teide ❿, picturesquely surrounded by vineyards and cornfields, nestles among the foothills of Teide and the Teno Mountains. Several large wine presses (*lagars*) rotting away at the side of the road make it clear that we're in a wine region. A few pleasant stores on the main road and a tasting center cater to the tourists. At the center of Santiago there's a Moorish-style whitewashed church, built in the early 20th century, with a small domed roof. A pass road in front of it leads off to the west, and to one of the landscape highlights of Tenerife: first of all there's a fantastic view from the top of the pass, the ***Degollada de Cherfe**, back down across the Santiago Valley, dominated majestically by the summit of Teide. You can clearly see the black tongues of lava from the last eruption here, up on the Teide Massif. Across to the west and the north are the jagged Teno Mountains, La Gomera can be seen across the ocean, and in good weather you can even make out La Palma to the northwest. Don't miss this amazing panorama. It's not far from here to Tenerife's most attractive village, either!

**Masca – Finest Village on the Island

A narrow, winding road leads to ****Masca** ⓫, the location of which re-

sembles the bottom of a well-shaft. It consists of several small hamlets; their houses are made of natural dark stone and are located on the few relatively flat areas of the rocks. A series of pleasant restaurants fits into the landscape nicely, so you can enjoy the excellent combination of delicious food and amazing panoramic view. Before the tourist boom this place was considered by many to be the finest village on the island, and could only be reached along mule paths. These days it's far too overcrowded with visitors, because the **Barranco de Masca** has become a very popular place in which to go hiking.

The hike down the winding path into the ravine is one of the most exciting things you can do on Tenerife. Depending on your stamina it can take from two to three hours (and almost twice as long to get back up), but the weird ravine rewards all the trouble you take with a whole series of plants endemic to the island, all of which are protected. On hot afternoons the air here can be incredibly hot – so don't forget to bring along enough to drink. When the tide is out a black beach appears by the sea, but swimming in strong surf is very dangerous, and there are also hidden rocks beneath the water. If you don't feel like making the tiring return journey, you can arrange for a fisherman from Playa de Santiago to pick you up in advance – just decide on a price and a time with him.

Above and Right: The hike through the bizarre Barranco de Masca (above) from the picturesque village of Masca (right) is now one of the most popular hiking routes on Tenerife.

If you don't feel all that athletic, a less arduous hike leads to a deserted farmstead, the **Finca de Guergues**. It is located on a sloping plateau to the south of the Barranco de Masca and affords impressive views of the Barranco Seco and as far as Las Américas. You start the hike near the **Casas de Araza**, visible directly below from the Degollada de Cherfe, and stay on the path which first leads up to the southern edge of the Barranco de Masca

Map pp. 16-17, Info pp. 53-59

so you can get several great views of its depths. On foot, one way, this trip takes around two hours. The former threshing floor is a good place to have a picnic.

In the Teno Mountains

A well-paved road with a few dangerous narrow sections leads up to the top of the pass, beyond which you'll see the high valley of **El Palmar**. There are a few hamlets dotted across this broad green valley, with its wonderful scent of eucalyptus and wild fennel. The area's main town, El Palmar, nestles beneath a volcanic cone which has bits cut out of it in several places, rather like a cake, to provide fertile volcanic earth for the banana plantations.

From El Palmar the journey continues westwards to a high plateau and to **Teno Alto**. Although there's actually a restaurant here now as well as a store, this place is like going back hundreds of years. The farmers in the small hamlets around here, who have to make do with a few goats and a tiny plot of land, do not have an easy time of things. It's not surprising that a lot of young people are deserting the villages up here. The old people use scythes to cut animal fodder from the roadside and then carry the heavy bundles home on their heads, accompanied by their dogs. By the way, there's a great route through this unspoiled landscape for weatherproof hikers: a path leads slightly downhill from Teno Alto and westwards to the edge of the Teno Massif, from where you can see the lighthouse on the Punta de Teno; and you can also reach it via a steep path that goes down the edge of the massif (about five hours there and back).

Back in El Palmar, keep traveling north and go down the coast as far as **Buenavista**, a town still largely untouched by tourism. There's a small harbor for fishing boats here, and the **Playa de los Barcos** with its rough pebble beach sometimes gets visited by tourists. The large village square has an inviting coffee pavilion for a well-earned rest. This is the other, peaceful side of Tenerife, where

time oftens seems to be standing still. The nearby **Iglesia Nuestra Señora de los Remedios**, built in 1513 and the most important historic building in Buenavista, was unfortunately destroyed in a fire in 1996. Renovators are trying to reconstruct the interior again, with its fascinating *mudéjar* ceiling.

If the road happens not to be closed because of rain, there's a good detour at this point to the lighthouse on the **Punta de Teno**. Travel along this spectacular steep coast and through two tunnels, and you'll reach the **Faro de Teno** and several small bays that are used for swimming when the sea is calm, despite a rather uncomfortable descent to get there. The color contrast between the crystal-clear turquoise of the sea and the reddish-brown volcanic rock is also very pleasant, even if swimming isn't possible.

Above: The whole place relaxes during a Romería, here in Buenavista. Right: Garachico – architectural jewel in the northwest of Tenerife.

East of Buenavista, in the midst of banana plantations, is **Los Silos** ⓬, which like the entire northwestern corner of Tenerife has fortunately remained largely undiscovered by tourism as yet. People don't come to Los Silos for impressive sights, nor for the rather eclectic, wedding-cake-style church of **Nuestra Señora de la Luz**. They come here for the idyllic and shady square at the center of the village with the obligatory coffee pavilion in the middle – all of it reached along a bumpy road.

For hikers, the **Laurel Forest** in the mountains to the south of Los Silos is a real treat. Leave the village at the church and soon you'll pass through a deserted hamlet called **Cuevas Negras**, where "hippies" (the name the locals give to dropouts) sometimes live. At Los Erjos on the high road, curve away to the west in order to get back to Los Silos. This round hike, which takes all day, leads through the largest intact laurel forest on the island and is an unforgettable experience for nature lovers.

*Garachico – Past Glory

***Garachico** ⓭ is a real jewel. Hardly any other place on the island has remained so homogeneously intact as this town, which was once the largest trading harbor on the island. In 1706, the wealthy little community was rendered totally insignificant after the worst volcanic eruption in the island's history: lava poured through large parts of the town, burying whole districts and much of the harbor. Garachico never recovered economically from this catastrophe – but it still has several houses in the simple, traditional style and several historic buildings as well, and overall presents a rare picture of architectural unity.

Even before you reach the town – by the bend in the road with the **Monumento al Emigrante Canario** ("Monument to the Canarian Emigrant"), where the statue has a hole in its chest in place of its heart – you will see the central parish church of **Santa Ana**. Its predecessor was destroyed by fire in the 1706 eruption, approximately 200 years after it was first built, but today's church still contains the first retables ever made on the island – because an artists' workshop for altarpieces has been doing good business in prosperous Garachico ever since the 17th century.

Beyond the church is the shady **Plaza de Arriba** with its monument in honor of Simón Bolívar, liberator of South America, and the pavilion so typical of the island. The gloomy-looking **Palacio de los Condes de la Gomera** ("Palace of the Counts of Gomera"; 17th century) is made of dark-gray basalt, and looks like it could do with some renovation work. It takes up almost the whole south side of the square.

The **Convento de San Francisco** (Franciscan monastery, 16th century) on the **Plaza Glorieta de San Francisco** is now a cultural center, and is also worth a visit. Its rooms contain alternating exhibitions of works by local artists. Photographs and documentation about the town's history are on display here, to-

gether with several liturgical instruments and a collection of stuffed sea animals, birds and butterflies.

The former harbor gate, or **Puerta de Tierra**, was dug out of the section of harbor that was buried by the lava, and is now surrounded by an attractive park. Hidden away in back of it is an old wooden wine press, and the **Castillo de San Miguel** (17th century) is a relic from the days of pirates. Once built to defend the harbor, it now contains an interesting exhibition of rocks, fossils and shells. On the terrace next door you can enjoy a meal with a view of the seawater swimming pool, best appreciated at sunset.

On the eastern edge of town is the former **Dominican Monastery**, which today is an old people's home. The chapel attached to it is a museum of modern art, and numerous works by local artists can be seen here. Concerts here are highly recommended by the way; it's certainly hard to think of a better setting for chamber music.

Above: This attractive Canarian balcony in Icod de los Vinos clearly shows Andalusian influence. Right: The main attraction in Icod de los Vinos is the Drago Milenario, seen here with San Marcos in the background.

Hikers who also like history will enjoy the cobbled former bridle path that leads to **San Juan del Reparo**, and which starts beyond the harbor park. The two-hour walk provides hikers with a rewarding view of Garachico, towering above the sea like a huge balcony of lava.

Icod de los Vinos

Ancient myths relate that the first settlers here in the pre-Hispanic era arrived on the island close to the region around today's **Icod de los Vinos** ⓮, 200 meters above the sea. Located right beneath the peak of Teide, the town gets an awe-inspiring view of the "Fujiyama of the Canaries."

Icod de los Vinos, as its name suggests, is surrounded by a very fertile wine growing region. Efforts made over past years to keep quality steady have won this region the right to a special indication of region of origin (*Ycoden Daute Isora*). The undisputed main attraction in Icod, however, is its legendary dragon tree known as the ***Drago Milenario**, which, though reputed to be 1,000 years old, is probably "only" half that age. Despite all its concrete and metal supports it is still very much alive, however. Since a dragon tree isn't really a proper tree at all, its real age can't be measured by counting its rings. There is no more mighty specimen of this endemic plant anywhere else in the Canary Islands, however. The tree was sacred to the Guanches, who used its sap for curative purposes and embalmed their dead with it, and today it is a protected species.

On the church square and the nearby Plaza de la Constitución there are more interesting plants, including ornamental banana and jacaranda. The three-aisled

Map pp. 16-17, Info pp. 53-59

***Iglesia San Marcos** (15th-century) with its late Gothic, Renaissance and Baroque elements contains fine retables and Artesonado ceilings. Its church treasure includes liturgical implements, Mass clothing and a cross made of Mexican silver. It weighs 47 kilograms and is two meters high, and is thought to be the largest filigree silver cross ever made (on display in the mornings in the sacristy).

The **Plaza de la Constitución**, located a little higher up, still looks the same as it did 200 years ago. With its centuries-old traditional-style buildings and its mossy well in the middle, it's one of the most homogeneous places on the island. Wine-tasting cellars and shops selling wines and cheeses from the region ensure that visitors can feast more than their eyes on what this place has to offer.

Every year on the night of November 29 the town comes alive. The bodegas celebrate the end of the wine harvest, and there's a big fiesta out in the streets with hot chestnuts, barbecued meat on skewers and plenty of wine to wash it all down. Young people race down the steep streets of Icod on improvised wooden sleds at amazing speeds. Although a high pile of car tires brakes their descent at the bottom, the crazier ones always race past and often get injured quite badly.

The ***Playa de San Marcos** is a far quieter place altogether, indeed it's one of the safest swimming bays in the north. The black sand beach lies below the town, and is protected by enormous rocky projections. In the summer most of the visitors here are locals, but in the winter they find the water too cold, and leave the tourists to themselves.

Anyone who wants to go back from Icod de los Vinos southwards will find themselves on a high road that leads through several hamlets to **El Tanque** and from there, via the 1,100-meter-high **Puerto de Erjos** pass, into the high valley of Santiago del Teide (see p. 23). On the western edge of El Tanque Alto (the upper section of the village), on the road to Tierra del Trigo, there's a *mirador* with a good view of Teide and the coast. A cooking school restaurant here is a good place to stop and enjoy some fine Canarian food. The simple Canarian-style building on the turnoff to the observation point with the bizarre sculptures serves as a studio for the Italian artist Antoine Manfredi.

From Icod de los Vinos, the round-trip tour of the island can either run along the main route, which leads directly to the highway at Puerto de la Cruz, or along a rather more complicated mountain route that passes through La Guancha to La Orotava, located in the higher reaches of the Orotava Valley.

On the coast road from Icod to the Orotava Valley, you'll pass a series of small villages, with restaurants and stopping off places. The larger villages are off to the side closer to the sea – one of these is **San Juan de la Rambla**, a nice place with a recently refurbished center. The church and surrounding buildings have all been newly whitewashed, and many houses still have old Canarian wooden balconies, shady patios and red tiled roofs.

One of these buildings has been rented out by an international group of artists, who have founded the **Biblioteca Expresión Contemporánea Antonín Artaud**, in which exhibitions, lectures, discussions and workshops are held. If you're interested in local art, this is one of the top addresses.

The country road leads into a rural region just after Icod and then up to **La Guancha**, and is far less traveled than the coastal route. Leaving the modern and rather too tidy village behind you, drive up to the observation point on the **Ladera de Tigaiga**, just after Icod El Alto. Here you'll see the entire Orotava Valley at your feet. Once praised by German naturalist and writer Alexander von Humboldt for its gentleness and varied flora, this strip of land is now one of the most built-up on Tenerife. There's a larger-than-life statue of Bentor here, the son of the Mencey of Taoro, who jumped off the edge of the Ladera to his death after the Guanches were defeated at La Victoria del Acentejo (see p. 35).

Right: Flowers carpeting the streets and festive flags and pennants at all the windows mark the route of Orotava's Corpus Christi procession.

THE OROTAVA VALLEY

Although **Los Realejos** ⓯ seems close enough to touch from the Mirador, there are several more hairpin bends to negotiate before you reach the upper part of it (Realejo Alto). Realejo Bajo and several settlements down near the coast combine with Realejo Alto to make up Los Realejos, the name of which is derived from the Spanish conquerors' royal camp (*real* = "royal"). Even though this is an old town – it was one of the first towns founded by the island's new overlords – the atmosphere is anything but old-fashioned. Both historic sections of it are full of modern buildings, and the churches are now almost the only reminder of its past. It was in today's lower town that the Spaniards finally managed to break the resistance of the Guanches of Taoro, and the defeated aboriginal population was forced to be baptized in the upper town.

The **church** in the upper town was completed as long ago as 1498, and is therefore the oldest on Tenerife. It was built on the site of Alonso de Lugo's military camp. The choir at the main altar is 17th-century, but not much remains of the church's original structure now. A tower was added in 1774 during one of the frequent periods of alteration work. Highlights inside the building include a statue of Christ by Martín de Andújar, and a Flemish *Santa Lucía*.

Outside the church is a monument honoring the cleric and thinker José Viera y Clavijo (1731-1813), the town's most

famous native son, who was the first person to write a detailed history of the Canary Islands, the *Noticias de la Historia General de las Islas Canarias,* which has been the official work of reference for the past two centuries. Clavijo, an enlightened theologian and a friend of Voltaire and other free thinkers, died in Las Palmas in 1813.

*La Orotava – Old Trading Town Steeped in History

At the eastern end of the Orotava Valley, 400 meters above the sea, lies the town of ***La Orotava** ⓰. The showpiece of this fast-growing municipality is its well-preserved historic ***Old Town**, all of which has been put under a preservation order. This is also where most visitors come, rather than to the busy eastern part of town with all its stores, apartment blocks and industrial estates. The old Town Hall square is still the center of life here. The famous carpet of colorful volcanic earth and blossoms is laid out here and in the narrow lanes along the path of the annual Corpus Christi procession.

Orotava's Old Town, which reveals just how wealthy the merchants in this municipality were in former days, is best explored from the **Plaza de la Constitución**. Enjoy a coffee in the pavilion, and the view of the remarkable buildings around the square. The former **Augustinian Convent**, dating from the 17th century, has a freshly renovated monastery church containing retables (shelves or frames enclosing decorated panels behind altars) from various epochs and an artistic Artesonado ceiling.

The **Liceo de Taoro**, reminiscent of an Italian country house, was formerly a school and today is used as a casino by a private cultural association. To the right, beyond the Liceo, you can see the marble mausoleum of the Ponte family (designed by French artist Adolphe Coquet in 1882) in the **Jardín Victoria**, a renovated public park. The view of the old section of La Oratava from the mausoleum is the best in town.

To the west of the plaza stands the Baroque **Iglesia Nuestra Señora de la Concepción**. It was built in 1788 above the foundations of a previous structure that was destroyed by an earthquake in 1705. The church contains a fine *Dolorosa* and a statue of St. John by José Luján Pérez from Gran Canaria; the *Candelaria* and St. Peter statues are by Fernando Estévez, a native of La Orotava. The neoclassical marble pulpit is Genoese, and the marble tabernacle on the main altar is by the Italian master Giuseppe Gagini. There are also two very good paintings: *The Marriage of the Virgin Mary to St. Joseph* by Cristóbal Quintana, and an *Immaculate Conception* by Gaspard de Quevedo.

Many of the townhouses and manors in La Orotava proudly bear familial coats of arms carved in stone above their main doorways. Some of the historic buildings have long balconies of dark Canary pine, and have shady patios and wooden verandas surrounded by much luxuriant foliage. Good examples of these can be found in the steep Calle San Francisco at the 17th-century ***Casa de los Balcones** (above the church). Inside the houses, various Canarian craft products are on display and for sale.

Above: The patio of the Casa de los Balcones in Orotava. Right: Puerto de la Cruz – coastal resort with a cosmopolitan character.

There are simpler houses from earlier epochs in the mill district of **Farrabo** above the Old Town. Even though the old watermills have been replaced by motorized ones, many of the old implements still survive and are happily shown to visitors. The mills can be recognized by their round structure, and usually (but not always) have damaged-looking water pipes leading to them.

On the way from the Casas de los Balcones to the Town Hall is **El Pueblo Guanche**, a small ethnographical museum inside a renovated townhouse. The Canarian food served here in traditional surroundings is almost more remarkable than the exhibition of finds from the pre-Hispanic era.

Behind the neoclassical Town Hall is a park called **Hijuela**. It is part of the Botanical Gardens of Puerto de la Cruz, which has plants native to the Canary Islands, as well as several species that were introduced later.

Back at the Plaza de la Constitución, you can see the church tower of the Monastery of Santo Domingo towering above the jumble of rooftops. If you're keen on seeing a very nice museum, visit the ***Museo de Artesanía Iberoamericana** inside this attractively restored monastery building. Several exhibition halls on two levels contain collections of Latin-American musical instruments, ceramics, woven products, textiles and a series of prize-winning items of furniture designed by local artists.

The upper Orotava Valley is an ideal place for lonely walks and long hikes. Good starting points are **La Caldera**, a

Map pp. 16-17, Info pp. 53-59

picnic site inside a small crater, or the nearby **Aguamansa** with its fishponds. It's also rewarding to go on a roughly three-hour-long tour around Los Órganos, a rock formation resembling organ pipes that you can see peeking through the trees at La Caldera. Another possibility is to follow the pilgrim route to Arafo (about five hours), signposted 200 meters to the east of La Caldera, which leads along the Cumbre Dorsal and down to the south.

Puerto de la Cruz – Bastion of Tourism

From a distance **Puerto de la Cruz** ⓱ may appear rather forbidding because of the endless line of horrid skyscrapers along the coast. Nevertheless, the former harbor of La Orotava has retained a few little corners that visitors have kept returning to over the years. The harbor is used by just a handful of fishermen, whose boats provide a welcome dash of color against the grayish-black pebble shore. Beyond the harbor, the crowded **Plaza del Charco**, with its shady Indian laurel, is definitely the heart of the town.

Across to the west is the most unspoiled quarter, **La Ranilla**, with its small but excellent restaurants. The main tourist street begins over to the east. It leads past the **Iglesia San Francisco** (1608), which is used as an art gallery today, and the slightly elevated church square to the **Punta del Viento**, where a short promenade above the steep coast begins. From here you can see the ***Lago Martiánez**, the seawater swimming pool designed by César Manrique using only natural materials from the island. The tourist street ends at the newly-created **Playa de Martiánez**, where restaurants playing international pop oldies suddenly seem to be all over the place.

Relics from the time when Puerto rose to become the most important trading harbor in the northern part of the island after the destruction of Garachico can be found all over this tourist center. From west to east they are the **Castillo San**

Felipe (early 17th century), which puts on good exhibitions and has even better concerts than the Playa Jardín; the former **Customs House** at the harbor; severable respectable-looking merchants' houses, such as the **Casa Iriarte** on Calle San Juan; or the town villas that have now become the **Marquesa** and **Monopol** hotels.

The two hotels stand opposite the ***Iglesia Nuestra Señora de la Peña de Francia**, a church popular for weddings. This church, with the small park beside it and the swan fountain in the plaza, is especially picturesque on moonlit nights. Inside it, local artist Luís de la Cruz has created paintings for retables and pulpits; there is also a *Dolorosa* by José Luján Pérez and a statue of St. Peter by Fernando Estévez.

One recent jewel is the wild and romantic ***Playa Jardín** in the west, which was designed by César Manrique. This black sand beach has brought Puerto de la Cruz a new clientele: while surfers display their talents offshore, people can bathe in the gentle surf, protected by submerged breakwaters. The park-like area beyond is a real eye-opener.

Above: Puerto de la Cruz is a great place to indulge in Mediterranean-style food. Right: The dolphin show in the Loro Parque.

Just a short distance away to the southwest in the suburb of Punta Brava is the internationally-renowned ***Loro Parque**. This efficiently-run 125,000 square meter "parrot park" contains the largest parrot collection in the world, with over 300 species and sub-species. The entrance hall contains an "original" Thai village, while a Gambian market on the site gives the whole place an African feel. Roller-skating parrots show off their skills in the animal performances here, and there are also shows featuring sea lions and dolphins. A shark aquarium which can be walked through along a transparent underwater tunnel is a special attraction of the park.

Those more interested in plants should visit the ***Jardín de Aclimatación de**

Orotava in the La Paz district. This botanical garden was originally an intermediate storage location for tropical plants, which it was hoped could be trained to weather the climate of mainland Spain. As you can see, the plants are really flourishing here in Puerto, while in Spain they regularly withered away.

If you feel like leaving the hustle and bustle of Puerto de la Cruz and finding a nice, quiet and relaxing beach, go to **El Rincón** east of the town and walk down into the rocky bay at **Playa Bolullo**, with its beautiful black sand beach. No one knows how long this serene little place will last because investors are already planning a vacation complex with a golf course for the region.

On the edge of the Orotava Valley is **Santa Úrsula ⓲**, one of the sunniest towns in the north, and located on a busy through route. Innumerable stores, restaurants, banks, drugstores and repair shops have settled here. One of the few remaining historic buildings is the **parish church** dating from 1628, which contains a sculpture of St. Rita by Fernando Estévez. At the **Humboldt View**, an observation point halfway to Santa Úrsula, you can read the praises heaped on this region by the famous German scholar as you peer down on this still to some extent gentle-looking valley.

Traveling Through the Acentejo

Travel through the Acentejo and you are moving through a very important historical region: this is where the decisive and dramatic war of resistance between the Guanches and their Spanish conquerors was played out. The first village on the route, **La Victoria del Acentejo**, derives its name from the Spanish victory. Decimated by disease and exhausted from their long struggle, the Guanches were forced to surrender on Christmas Day in 1495. A wind-blown pine tree next to the church (above the main road) is thought to date from that time. Inside the church there's an artistic Artesonado ceiling in the *mudéjar* style, and the architecture of the main chapel is Portuguese-colonial. Several families in the village itself are continuing the tradition of pottery making without the use of a wheel, as practiced by the Guanches.

The martial-sounding name of the neighboring village to the northeast, **La Matanza del Acentejo ⓳**, refers to the last victory of the Guanches before they were finally subjugated. The "bloodbath" of Acentejo, as the Spanish refer to their defeat, relates to a legend whereby the Guanches were not only very tough warriors but very cunning ones as well. Apparently they lured the Spanish into an ambush, and then broke up their battle lines by whistling loudly, thus getting a herd of goats to charge among them. After the hail of lances and rocks had ended the Spaniards had lost 900 mercenaries, the majority of them Canarian. The Spanish conqueror Alonso de Lugo was very lucky to escape alive.

THE NORTHEAST COAST AND ANAGA MOUNTAINS

The backbone of the northeast is formed by the Anaga Mountains, with fertile valleys to the west and northwest. The coastline in this part of Tenerife is rough and unsuitable for swimmers; hikers and wine lovers are more in their element around here. The latter should definitely visit **El Sauzal**, with its attractive ensemble consisting of the Neo-Canarian Town Hall with its large flight of steps and the domed white church. There's a great view of the steep northern coast from the church square and also from an observation point just below it.

Just outside this town, near the highway exit, there's another jewel in the shape of the ***Casa del Vino**. This renovated country house in the La Baranda district is a center of Tenerife wine, which goes extremely well with the substantial Canarian food. This blend of museum, wine-tasting hall, bar, restaurant and store was voted the best restaurant on Tenerife by the island's newspapers in 1995.

Right: The Anaga Mountains are a paradise for hikers.

The busiest wine town around here is **Tacoronte ⓴** on the far western edge of the high plateau of La Laguna (500 meters above sea level). Its vintners have had their wine officially recognized and were the first on the island to fulfill the EU norms. **Bodegas Álvaro**, with its large selection of wines, organizes tastings and is visited by numerous bus groups. The building is two kilometers outside the town center on the road to La Laguna, and is definitely worth a brief stopover if you feel like familiarizing yourself with the archipelago's greatest wines.

The two church squares are oases of peace in this busy small town. The churches that go with them – the **monastery church** of the Augustinian Order near the center and the **Iglesia Santa Catalina** located a little lower down, are the most important sights to be seen around here. The ornamentation on the retables inside reveals a distinctly Latin-American influence.

Mesa del Mar and **El Pris**, two small towns on the coast reached via steep roads, should be visited by anyone who really enjoyed the view of the steep coast near El Sauzal. While the cliffs are far more attractive than the buildings in Mesa del Mar, El Pris is a sleepy little fishing village which unfortunately has not totally escaped the tourist trade. Beyond the large tunnel in Mesa del Mar there is a sheltered bay with black volcanic sand that is especially suitable for families with children who want to swim.

Valle de Guerra, in the steep valley of the same name, is surrounded by agriculture of all kinds, from banana plantations to fields of cut flowers. On its outskirts there is an agrarian institute researching into possibilities of improvement in culti-

Map pp. 16-17, Info pp. 53-59

vation methods so that they suit conditions on the island better. Nearby is the **Museo Etnográfico de Tenerife**, housed in an old building dating from the 17th century; it provides a glimpse into what country life was like in the past.

Also very agricultural is **Tejina ㉑**, on the eastern edge of the Valle de Guerra. Until the 1950s sugar cane was the main crop here, and was used to make rum in the local factory *Cocal*. Rum production is still here today (the factory is in the lower part of the town, and can produce up to 70,000 liters a day during its three-month season), but these days the sugar cane is imported from South Africa. The factory also produces the delicious, sweet "honey rum" (*ron miel*) as well as a banana liqueur.

From Tejina you can reach two resorts by the sea, which are mostly frequented by Germans. **Bajamar** with its large seawater swimming pool is a popular meeting place for the young people from nearby La Laguna. Not far away you can sit and watch the fishermen bringing in their catch. Otherwise there's not a lot going on here – but it appears to be just what the regular visitors here from Europe seem to like.

Punta del Hidalgo, at the foot of the Anaga Mountains, looks more touristy because of its high-rises on the coast, but that doesn't make it any more attractive. Here, too, things are amazingly quiet: all you can hear is the sound of the surf and the occasional shriek of a seagull. Two seawater swimming pools and a beach promenade form the center of the holiday action here. The main road leads to a raised round tower, from which there is a good view of the jagged coastline, and also of a valley in the Anaga Mountains with the double rock formation of **Roque Dos Hermanos** at its eastern end. A well-marked hiking route leads from here to the still-inhabited cave dwellings at Chinamada, where the houses and apartment blocks peering over the top of the mountain ridge are actually set into the rockface behind. The ascent takes two and half hours or so, but provides great

views of the steep coastline and the bays below. To continue the journey you have to go back to Tejina and then turn off southeastwards in the direction of **Tegueste**, which has one of the best wrestling teams in the Canaries for the local sport of *lucha canaria*. The large arena says it all.

Along the Ridges of the Anaga Mountains

A left turn near Lass Canteras leads into the green heart of the Anaga Mountains, with their wild, jagged peaks and deep valleys. A small village is followed by the forest of the same name, **Las Mercedes**, one of the densest laurel forests (*laurisilva*) in the Canaries. It blends into a bush-like plant formation known as *Fayal-Brezal*, the characteristic plants of which are the Dutch myrtle (*faya*) and the brier (*brezo*).

Above: Lucha canaria in Tegueste. Right: The Playa de las Teresitas.

A series of observation points now follow along the winding road: the **Miradores Jardín** and **Cruz del Carmen** provide very good views across the plain of La Laguna and Teide in fine weather.

The panoramic view from the ***Pico del Inglés** ㉒, however, is unbeatable: from here, at an altitude of around 1,000 meters, you can look in every direction, across the green valleys and rough coastline around the Anaga Mountains – that is assuming there are no trade-wind clouds shrouding the scenery, which often happens after 11 a.m. There's a slightly more limited view from the drafty ridge of the **Bailadero**: to the south you can see part of the harbor installations at Santa Cruz de Tenerife, to the north you'll see **Taganana**, a picturesque village, with thin rows of white houses against the green of the valley. The heavy *Mavasía* grape is still grown here – the high altitude saved the vines from destruction during the phylloxera epidemic.

Down by the sea, on a weird-looking rocky outcrop, is the hamlet of **Roque de**

Map pp. 16-17, Info pp. 53-59

las Bodegas, which consists almost exclusively of seafood restaurants. It's best not to go swimming on the sand-and-pebble beach here with the rocks in between, though some surfers are actually attracted by the big waves.

If you want to explore the eastern Anaga Mountains, travel back to El Bailadero and go to the end of the road from there to **Chamorga** ㉓. This town is the starting point for an extremely varied, day-long hike around the northeastern tip of Tenerife, which will take you through El Draguillo, Las Palmas and Roque Bermejo.

In good weather, walking among the great variety of plant and rock formations, you'll be able to see the entire Anaga coastline. Apart from a long, slow climb at the end, this hike is well-marked and can easily be undertaken by the reasonably fit. Bring food and drink along, however, because there are no places to buy anything along the way.

You can reach the capital, Santa Cruz de Tenerife, by taking the coast road via **San Andrés** ㉔. This small fishing village with its simple white houses is visited either for its excellent seafood or for a swim. Situated at the end of the 10-kilometer-long harbor installation of Santa Cruz, San Andrés formerly had the job of securing the northeastern flank of the capital in times of trouble. A collapsed watchtower stands as a reminder of that time.

On weekends or after work the *chicharreros*, as the people of the capital call themselves, come and have fun on the long, palm-lined ***Playa de las Teresitas**. A breakwater made of moss-covered stones allows people to bathe in peace, and protects the beach with its yellow sand which was imported here from the Sahara Desert. Showers are placed at regular intervals along the beach. Restaurants behind the beach area provide tapas and fresh drinks, and in the evenings the seafood restaurants along the Avenida Marítima in San Andrés are very popular. The fish is usually fresh, but to make absolutely sure it's best to eat at restaurants that keep live fish swimming outside their doors in aquariums.

*SANTA CRUZ DE TENERIFE
The New Metropolis

***Santa Cruz de Tenerife** ㉕, with its population of 200,000, is the largest town on the island and the second largest of the archipelago. It jointly runs the autonomous region of the Canary Islands together with the larger Las Palmas de Gran Canaria. Unlike Las Palmas, Santa Cruz de Tenerife has a far more harmonious appearance. This is largely because of its amphitheater-like location, framed as it is against the towering peaks of the Anaga Mountains.

At the heart of this semicircular city panorama is the **Plaza de España** ❶. If a large social event is about to occur – whether it's an open-air concert or a carnival – you can be sure it will take place here in this partly traffic-free square by the sea.

The Historic City Center

In the middle of the Plaza de España is the cruciform **Monumento a los Caídos**, in memory of all the Civil War dead of the island who fell fighting on the side of Franco. It was designed as an observation tower, and the plinth contains a small remembrance chapel. The tower has been closed ever since it became a May Day target for Canarian separatists in the 1970s so that, unfortunately, it cannot be climbed. Southwest of the monument is the **Palacio Insular** with its clock tower. Built in the eclectic style of the 1930s, it contains the island council (*Cabildo Insular*) and the tourist information office. The post and telegraph office to the right of it is housed inside a similarly monumental structure.

Beyond the Plaza de España, towards the center of the city, is a gently sloping square dedicated to the patron saint of the archipelago, the light-giving Madonna of the Candelaria. In the representative **Plaza de la Candelaria** ❷, with its fountain and numerous palm trees, there are several attractive street cafés. The lower part of the plaza is dominated by the **Triunfo de la Candelaria**, a monument in white Italian marble portraying four Guanche princes *(menceyes)* who collaborated with the Spanish worshiping the Madonna. On the northeastern side of the square is the **Casino de Tenerife**, an exclusive gentlemen's club where the most high-ranking members of the civic administration meet up. To the left of the modern Plaza Hotel is the **Palacio de los Rodríguez Carta**. This former townhouse, built in 1742, is now occupied by a

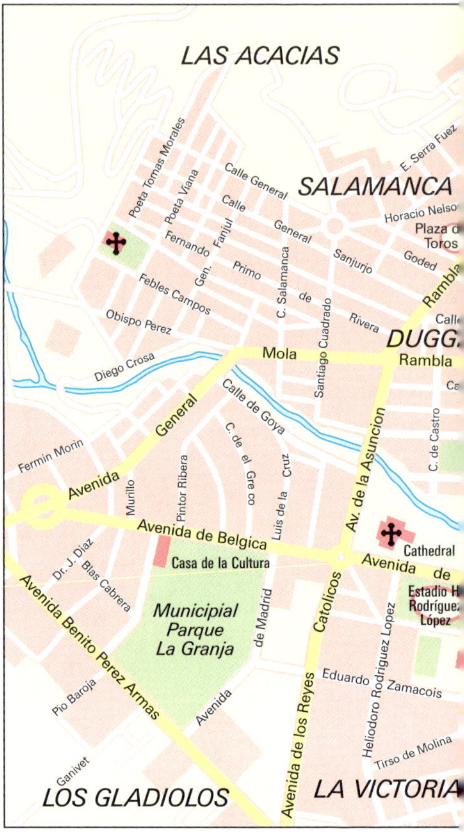

Map pp. 16-17, Info pp. 53-59

bank. The noble patio, with its verandas and staircases of dark Canary pine, can be admired during opening hours.

On **Calle del Castillo** a little farther on, there is one store after the next. As you stroll through this narrow pedestrian precinct with its attractive window displays, keep in mind that the stores (not the cafés) close between 1 and 4:30 p.m. The same applies to **Calle de Béthencourt Alfonso**, which runs parallel and also leads to the shadiest square in the capital, the **Plaza del Príncipe de Asturias** ❸. Under the impressive roof of mighty Indian laurels, the Café del Príncipe inside a fin-de-siècle-style glasshouse serves Canarian cakes, and concerts also take place here quite often.

The most striking-looking of the buildings around here is the clubhouse of the **Círculo de Amistad XII de Enero**, a private cultural association. Since it is not open to visitors you will have to content yourself with the sight of its eclectic early 20th-century facade with its dragons and female statues up on the gables. The **Museo Municipal** on the southeastern side of the square mainly contains works by local artists.

At the top end of Calle del Castillo you'll reach the **Plaza del General Weyler** ❹, with its noisy traffic and a marble fountain in the center called "The Well of Love" (*Fuente del Amor*) by the Genoese sculptor Achille Caresse. A more romantic place is the smaller **Plaza**

de los Patos ❺ on Avenida del 25 de Julio. Located at the center of an attractive villa area, this square – with its frog fountain and its Seville-tiled benches complete with nostalgic advertisements – is a very comfortable, quiet place to relax. South of it there is a row of government buildings that includes the seat of the Canarian president, the Bank of Spain, the Town Hall and the palazzo of the governor. The lime-green **Casa Quintero** ❻ at Calle Jesús y María 15, with its Art Nouveau stucco, is the most eye-catching building in this neighborhood.

It's not far now to the botanical gardens, also known as the ***Parque Municipal García Sanabria**. This six-hectare-large municipal park contains a vast number of plants, both endemic and imported. There are also leafy promenades, romantic trellises and splashing fountains, plus some bizarre items of modern sculpture – the relics of a public exhibition during the 1970s.

Above: The Plaza de España – heart of Santa Cruz. Right: The idyllic Plaza de los Patos on Avenida del 25 de Julio.

At the top end of the park you should walk a short way down the **Rambla del General Franco**. This avenue is where the locals meet up for their *paseo* after the siesta. As in the park, there are sculptures here dating from the 1970s, including a *Reclining Warrior* by Henry Moore.

Near the **floral clock** beside the lower entrance to the park you can recover nicely from your stroll in a café. The best way back to the Plaza de España is along **Calle de Pilar**, a shopping street with shops for elevated tastes.

Southwest of the City Center

If you take Avenida de Bravo Murillo southwestwards from the Plaza de España, you'll arrive at the freshly renovated **Iglesia de la Concepción** ❼. It was built in 1652 and is the successor of the town's first-ever church, built in 1502, which was destroyed in a fire. Its bell tower was also used as a lookout post, to

check whether pirates were around or anything was on fire. Typical features of Canarian architecture are the dark basalt stones on the tower and in the nave, and the balcony above the entrance. The octagonal tower served as a lookout post. Inside the low, five-aisled church the most noticeable features are the finely-carved Canary wood choir stalls and the various *mudéjar*-style ceilings. The Chapel of the Holy Heart, to the left of the altar, contains the cross carried by Alonso Fernández de Lugo when he claimed the islands. A further chapel contains the tombs of the islands' most famous classical composer, Teobaldo Power ("Cantos Canarios"), and General Gutiérrez, Lord Nelson's successful opponent.

On the other side of the Barranco de Santos is the building that housed the former hospital, and which today contains the ***Museo de la Naturaleza y el Hombre** ❽. This well-organized double museum has an archeological section displaying finds dating from the Guanche period, including some well-preserved mummies, and a natural history section with fossils, stones, and Canarian flora and fauna.

If you take a detour away from the city center, to the other side of Avenida 3 de Mayo, you can visit the **Parque Marítima** ❾: open-air swimming baths with a seawater pool and a South Seas atmosphere. Rather unfortunately, the park, designed according to plans by César Manrique, is located right next to a large oil refinery.

From the museum, go up Avenida de San Sebastián to the **Mercado de Nuestra Señora de África** ❿. In the mornings this place is a colorful jumble of stalls selling fish, fruit and vegetables, and is more akin to an Oriental bazaar than anything else. Outside the hall, food stands provide drinks and snacks. The market hall dates from the Franco period, and is supposed to have a stylized "Canarian village" look to it. On Sundays there's a large flea market all around the hall, which draws quite a few locals from round about. Handmade jewelry, mass-

produced junk and exotic imports all lie outside in the hot Canarian sunshine waiting for buyers. Beer and *café con leche* are served in the market halls.

On the way back into the center, just beyond the bridge over the Barranco de Santos, is the **Teatro Guimerá** ⓫, home of the Tenerife Symphony Orchestra. Numerous foreign artists perform here during the winter festival. The theater is named after the Catalan dramatist Ángel Guimerá, who was born here, and is used for theater, opera and ballet performances. Rather simple-looking on the outside, it has a great deal of Art Nouveau decoration inside.

Next door, in the **Centro de Fotografía**, housed inside a former market hall, there are alternating art and photographic exhibitions.

Above: A quick swig from a goatskin during a fiesta. Right: The pilgrimage destination of Santuario del Cristo on the northern edge of La Laguna contains a statue of Christ revered throughout the Canaries.

Calle Valentín Sanz will take you back to the city's pedestrian precinct for a well-earned rest at the Plaza del Príncipe.

*LA LAGUNA
The Old Capital

The island's former capital of San Cristóbal de La Laguna, now known as ***La Laguna** ㉖, is perched in a commanding position on the Aguere plateau, 500 meters above sea level. This sister city of Santa Cruz, with its cooler climate, has grown together with it. In 1496, immediately after the *Conquista*, the conqueror Alonso Fernández de Lugo had La Laguna built beside a lake as the capital of the island. In 1723, it lost this status (the lake dried up long beforehand), but to this day has remained the intellectual and religious center of the Canary Islands. The clearest sign of this is the university, which has been here since 1816 and was the only one on the entire archipelago until the end of the 1980s. Shortly after the university was founded in 1818,

City Map pp. 40-41, Info pp. 53-59

the town became a bishopric. The church and the university have controlled social and cultural life here ever since. The historic center is definitely worth a visit, and looks almost medieval with its narrow streets and numerous historic houses. Some of the ancient structures have been affectionately restored and are open to the public as museums.

The best starting point for a tour of La Laguna is the leafy ***Plaza del Adelantado** in the eastern part of the Old Town. This magnificent square is surrounded on all sides by historic buildings. To the east are the market and the law courts, and in between is the **Ermita San Miguel**, a monastery commissioned by the city's founders. Today it houses an art gallery.

At the southeastern corner of the square is the **Birthplace of Father Anchieta**, who went to Brazil as a missionary and founded the city of São Paulo. The neoclassical **Town Hall**, built in 1822, is to the right of it. To the left, on Calle Nava y Grimón, is the Neo-Gothic **Consistory** with its finials and foliage decoration, and across to the right of the square is the **Convento de Santa Catalina**. A wrought-iron balcony on one corner of the rather forbiddingly high wall is the most striking feature of this monastery, which dates from the early 17th century. The next building along is the Baroque **Palacio de Nava y Grimón**, a dark-gray palazzo dating from 1590 with a portico flanked by double columns. This was the home of an influential family of Canarian nobles during the Enlightenment.

If you carry on northeastwards along Calle de Nava y Grimón and then turn onto Calle San Agustín, you'll arrive at the ***Museo de Historia de Tenerife** in the **Casa Lercano**, another late-16th-century townhouse. The exhibition here is very good and centers around the history of the island since it was conquered.

Next, on the right, is a palazzo very similar in style to the Palacio de Nava y Grimón. It's the **Palacio Episcopal**, which was actually built half a century

later. The building, with its Baroque, gray basalt facade, was a casino for the town's prominent citizens before it became the episcopal palace. It was here that Canarian composer Teobaldo Power wrote his "Cantos Canarios."

Passing the mighty ruins of the late-15th-century **Convento de San Agustín**, take a narrow street to the left and you'll arrive at the oldest church in the city, the ***Iglesia de Nuestra Señora de la Concepción**. It dates from 1497, and owes its present appearance to various different late Gothic, Renaissance and Baroque alterations. The first subjugated Guanches were baptized in its glazed font, which was brought here from Seville. In the 16th century the church received its colorfully-painted Artesonado ceiling in the *mudéjar* style, part of which collapsed in 1972 and has since been replaced by a vaulted ceiling. The numerous impressive examples of Canarian woodcarving here include late Baroque statues of the Virgin by José Luján Pérez and Fernando Estévez, and also some fine carving on the pulpit and the choir stalls at the back.

Above: The Virgin of Candelaria, harbinger of Christianity and the patron saint of the archipelago. Right: Nine Menceyes, cast-bronze chieftains of the Guanches (Candelaria).

Take the main shopping street, Calle Obispo Rey Redondo, to get back to your starting point. On the way you'll pass the **Teatro Leal**, with a facade in the eclectic style of its architect Antonio Pintor.

The ***Catedral de los Remedios** stands on a small plaza behind high palm trees. The cathedral was built in 1511, while its neoclassical facade dates from 1820. Highlights inside the building include the gilt retable with paintings from the Flemish school, and the marble pulpit by Genoese sculptor Pasquale Bocciardo. Behind the altar is the tomb of the man who conquered Tenerife, Alonso Fernández de Lugo.

Before completing this stroll at the Town Hall on the Plaza del Adelantado, take a quick look at the **Casa de los Capitanes**. This former regent's palazzo contains some good exhibitions on the cultural history of the archipelago.

One of the most popular attractions of La Laguna is outside the city center in the direction of Santa Cruz: the ***Museo de la Ciencia y el Cosmos** belongs to the university, and is designed interactively so that it will appeal to children in particular. There are all kinds of buttons to press, computers, film rooms, and even a planetarium.

THE ARID SOUTH

The stretch of road that runs south from Santa Cruz is rather tedious at first glance: the landscape is often barren, and the monotony of earth colors is not even broken up by the odd green field. Nevertheless, this stretch does have its attractions, because this is a largely unknown side of Tenerife.

Map pp. 16-17, Info pp. 53-59

The highway south travels through the uninteresting suburbs of the capital as far as **Candelaria** ㉗. The main sight to see in this coastal town is the Neo-Canarian **Basílica de Nuestra Señora de Candelaria**, located right next to the sea. It contains the *Black Madonna of Candelaria*, a statue of the Virgin who is regarded as the patron saint of the archipelago. According to legend, the carved statue was washed up on the beach, and was worshiped for its miraculous powers by the Guanches who lived here long before they had contact with Christianity. The Spanish conquerors took advantage of this and won the Guanches of Güímar as allies against the Mencey of Taoro. The original statue, which could have come from the altar of a Portuguese ship, was washed into the sea after a tidal wave in the 19th century and never found again. The statue you see today is a copy of a copy that stands in the Pilar church in Santa Cruz.

On the side of the huge square outside the basilica that faces the sea, you can see realistically rendered ***bronze statues** depicting the nine Menceyes from the time of the *Conquista*. These figures are present at the celebrations marking the end of a pilgrimage right across the island that takes place in mid-August each year, and in which the conversion of the so-called heathen Guanches to Christianity plays a central and symbolic role. The dark pebble beach just beyond the Guanche statues is not a good place for swimming, by the way; bathing here is okay if the water is calm, but don't venture out too far.

The road inland from Candelaria passes several partially cultivated fields on its way to **Arafo**. This small peaceful village on the eastern slopes of the Cumbre Dorsal has won several "best-kept village" awards. Its church square, in the shade of an old Indian laurel, has a coffee pavilion that is an excellent place to stop for a refreshing drink or a snack. Alternatively you can visit one of the village bakeries to try some delicious *truchas*, a form of ravioli.

The next village to the south, **Güímar** ㉘, has made quite a name for itself because of its delicious wines. It was in the early 1990s, however, that it really hit the headlines when several carefully terraced pyramids made from uncut stone were unearthed in the suburb of Chacona. The Norwegian Thor Heyerdahl managed to have the area sealed off and began a systematic scientific investigation. His friend, shipowner Fred Olsen, was delighted by the idea of an ethnographic park and bought the land. Open since the end of 1997, the **Museo Casa Chacona** contains fascinating information about Heyerdahl's theories about ancient cultures being interconnected.

The almost forgotten part of Tenerife begins near the **Mirador de Don Martín**. Piles of volcanic ash and lava border carefully terraced fields, and narrow little bridges bravely span eroded barrancos. For a while little canals run parallel to the road, carrying drinking water from the heights of Güímar to Las Américas.

The village of **Arico** ㉙ consists of several sections spread out along the main road, and the middle one, Arico el Nuevo, is worthy of note. This tiny jewel of a village, with its houses and cobbled streets, is situated incredibly picturesquely against a barranco. The pilgrimage church in the main village of Lomo de Arico was based on the one in Granadilla, and contains a Gothic statue of the Virgin which, legend has it, was once washed up on the beach near Porís de Abona.

After several more tiny hamlets and hairpin bends you'll arrive at **Granadilla de Abona** ㉚, which greets its visitors with the **Iglesia San Antonio de Padua** (1711). This ambitious village is playing its part in the tourist boom by delivering produce to the tourist centers along the coast. The area produces wine, tomatoes, peppers, potatoes and maize. Beyond San Miguel is the **Mirador de la Centinela**,

Above: Rural peace and quiet in Arico el Nuevo. Right: In May the normally barren landscape of the Cañadas becomes a majestic carpet of flowering shrubbery.

Map pp. 16-17, Info pp. 53-59

with more bizarre landscape to round off this route through the interior. The coastal strip is lined with what look like enormous molehills: volcanic cones, as far as the eye can see. The best time to look at this weird scene is at sunset, when the hills throw long shadows.

From the observation point you can also see the much-cultivated **Valle de San Lorenzo** in the west. Its fertile volcanic soil, sheltered location and plentiful supply of water from the mountains create ideal conditions for agriculture. The modern town of the same name is located on one of the oldest parts of the island, geologically speaking; far older than the central massif behind it to the north.

**LAS CAÑADAS AND **TEIDE
Top of the World

This tour to the top of Tenerife is the true "highlight" of any trip round the island. The sight of majestic Mount Teide, and of the seemingly infinite lava fields of the Cañadas, is quite unforgettable, and more varied and monumental than anywhere else in the Canary Islands.

Even when seen from the road, the lava has its own story to tell. Particularly rough and bizarrely shaped surfaces have been produced by lava with a higher gas content, while the shiny black glassy surfaces mark the areas that cooled down rapidly without having the time to crystallize. This black substance is known as obsidian, and the Guanches used it to make axe blades.

This is a superb hiking area. The massive, elliptical Caldera (sunken crater) is 17 kilometers long and 11 kilometers across, and is worth visiting at any time of the year. If the rather dry and barren landscape here in the fall doesn't appeal, come back in May when the lava fields are covered with pink, white and yellow flowers, and the air is full of the sound of honey bees. The experience is quite unforgettable. By the way, anyone who wants to spot a *moufflon* (it's a famously shaggy sheep) will need a pair of binoculars and a great deal of patience!

Reaching Teide by Car

Just outside Arona the people in charge of the *Parque Ecológico Las Águilas del Teide** have turned the stony desert into an artistic oasis most effectively. The crocodile pool, floodlit with various colors at night, is especially impressive. There are several feedings and shows every day, and highlights also include condors in flight. Variety shows in the evenings are also a regular attraction.

Anyone who reaches **Arona** ㉛, a village that was probably founded by an Italian, has well and truly escaped the tourist bustle of Tenerife. In front of the Neo-Canarian Town Hall is a shady and idyllic plaza, which suits the little village perfectly. The **Iglesia San Antonio** was built in the Spanish colonial style in 1627. Its retable is one of the finest in Spain and was brought here on mules from Adeje, when church property there was threatened with secularization. Arona lies at the eastern edge of the most striking mountain in the south, the 1,003-meter-high **Roque del Conde**. This sloping table mountain, popular as a starting point for paragliders, can easily be distinguished among the other volcanoes.

Above: Vilafor lace is homemade, and takes a long time to create. Right: The Teide echium, which can flower up to 80,000 times, is endemic to Tenerife.

A well-surfaced but winding road leads up to **Vilaflor** ㉜, often praised in old travel reports as a health resort for those with respiratory problems because of the many pine forests surrounding it. Located at an elevation of 1,400 meters it is not only the highest village in the Canaries but in all of Spain! A Mirador upon a steep hill to the west will help you get your bearings.

In the slightly sloping plaza in the upper part of the village you will see the small historic section, with the **Iglesia San Pedro** (1550), a ruined monastery and a former mill. On the hill behind the monastery, the people in charge of *Las Águilas del Teide* have set up a small **ad-**

Map pp. 16-17, Info pp. 53-59

venture park with a Guanche history **museum**. This village became famous for the fine lace produced by its women: Vilaflor Lace has been exported to Spain and overseas since the 19th century. Several old women in Vilaflor still know the technique, and their work is on sale.

Many hikers come to Vilaflor and the surrounding region each year. One very good tour from here leads across the so-called ***Paisaje Lunar** ("Lunar Landscape"), an eroded section of landscape that resembles Turkey's Cappadocia in miniature, and on into the Cañadas. If you want to see the lunar landscape without venturing any farther, follow a broad forest road six kilometers above Vilaflor as far as the start of a signposted hiking route. It's just half an hour's walk to the first weird rock formations.

If you continue farther into the Cañadas by car you'll pass through airy pine forests, and then get one of the most spectacular views of neighboring islands that Tenerife has to offer. At first, Gran Canaria to the east will be all you can see, but later on both La Gomera and El Hierro will appear in the southwest. Near the Boca del Tauce you'll finally arrive at the crater arena of the Cañadas, and at the 136-square-kilometer ****Teide National Park** ㉝.

**Teide National Park

****Las Cañadas**, made up of two levels of differing heights, is oval in shape, almost 17 kilometers long and 10 kilometers across. At some locations the crater walls reach elevations of 700 meters or more above the crater floor. From the very highest point, the **Guajara** (2,717 meters), there is an absolutely stunning view of the Cañadas and Teide. The stone desert of solidified lava, volcanic cones, pumice stone and bizarre rock formations has very distinctive vegetation, which has adapted to the very dry summers. It starts flowering in spring and

makes the Cañadas glow with all kinds of different colors for three months. In the winter snow falls, covering Teide and also the Cañadas with a white blanket for weeks on end.

On the right, beyond the Boca del Tauce and on the crater floor of the **Zapato de la Reina** ("Queen's Shoe"), there's a rock formation that is reminiscent of a high-heeled shoe. On the left is the **Llano de Ucanca**, an alluvial landscape that has been used in several science fiction movies. In the background you can see the Roques de García, reached via **Los Azulejos**; the turquoise colors on them are caused by iron.

The ***Roques de García** are among the strangest rock formations in the Cañadas; some of these are frozen rivers of volcanic vents, others are eroded structures with several layers. Nearby there's a **Parador Nacional** with a restaurant and a small museum documenting the national park.

Towering above all this, however, is the cone-shaped summit of ****Pico del**

Teide. The highest mountain in Spain (3,717 meters) has destroyed the north wall of the Caldera in its various eruptions, and completely buried it. Its older neighbor, ***Pico Viejo**, is 3,135 meters high and actually has a more impressive crater than Teide itself. The **Centro de Visitantes** ㉞ on the northeastern edge of the Cañadas provides video presentations (in English, Spanish and German) about the national park. You can also obtain information here on hiking routes, guided tours and accommodation at the *Altavista* mountain hut.

Teide can be ascended on foot, but to get to the actual summit via the Rambleta you'll need a permit (available from the *Patronato del Parque Nacional de las Cañadas del Teide* in Santa Cruz). The most popular route (five hours) starts at **Montaña Blanca** (2,750 meters) and first leads along a dirt track, passing pumice fields with the famous "Teide eggs," volcanic boulders as large as automobiles. A steep and winding path leads up to the newly-renovated *Altavista* mountain hut, almost 3,300 meters up, from which it takes around one more hour on foot to reach the Rambleta (3,560 meters). That's where the **Teleférico del Teide** cable railway comes in – its two gondolas arrive up here from a station located at an altitude of 2,356 meters, but only if there's no wind. For environmental reasons, only 150 people are allowed on the Rambleta at any one time, so if the weather is nice you can expect lengthy waits for the cable car.

Above: The oval crater arena in the Cañadas at the foot of Teide has a diameter of between 10 and 17 kilometers.

In **El Portillo** at the eastern end of the national park, at 2,000 meters above sea level, there are several restaurants. Beyond them you can drive down northwards into the Valle de la Orotava, where the pine and laurel forests in the upper section of the valley, with its moderate climate, are a very attractive place to go hiking (see pp. 30-31). If you turn east near El Portillo, you'll arrive at the

Cumbre Dorsal, a mountain ridge consisting of a chain of volcanoes that all merged into each other long ago. Near **Izaña** there are several white observatories keeping a regular eye on the universe.

Now you're on a pass road with views of the coastal strip on either side. Depending on the trade-wind cloud situation, you'll plunge from the sunny heights into a weird world of fog between 1,500 meters and 800 meters above sea level, and it often only dissipates once you get down to **La Esperanza** ㉟. This village is the main one in the scattered community of **El Rosario**, whose hamlets extend from the La Laguna plateau as far as the largely pine-filled **Bosque de la Esperanza**.

Ecologically, this forest is very important to the island. The long pine needles collect water from the clouds and the soil in the forest here therefore has three times the water content of other areas. Canary pine is more resistant to forest fires than other trees because of its thick, nearly impenetrable bark, and is also relatively impervious to extended periods of winter cold or summer drought. These advantages have been realized, and much reforestation is now under way using the endemic variety, rather than other faster-growing species which have proven unsuitable.

This area is famous for restaurants that serve large quantities of very filling food. Pork, veal and rabbit dishes are especially popular, but things tend to get crowded on weekends so make sure you book in advance. Apart from the restaurants along the access route to the Cañadas, however, this region has almost remained untouched by tourism: this is the true, unadulterated Tenerife. Popular spare-time activities up here include hikes through the Esperanza Forest, and barbecues and picnics at the special sites (but beware of forest fires!). Near La Laguna, down in the valley, a highway junction takes you back to the outside world.

TENERIFE

ARRIVAL: **By Plane:** International air traffic arrives at the *Aeropuerto Reina Sofía* in the south, and national flights arrive at *Tenerife Norte* (Los Rodeos near La Laguna). Charter flights are available from the UK the whole year round. **By Ship:** From *Los Cristianos* habor in the south there are daily ferry connections to La Gomera (90 mins.; hydrofoil 35 mins.), La Palma (4 hours) and El Hierro (5 hours). From the capital, *Santa Cruz* ships travel to Lanzarote (10 hours), Gran Canaria (3.5 hours; jetfoil 80 mins.), Fuerteventura (14 hours), La Palma (8 hours) and – once a week – to Cádiz on the Spanish mainland. Info: Lineas Fred Olsen, tel. 922-628200, and Trasmediterránea, tel. 902-454645. Internet: www.fredolsen.es / www.trasmediterranea.es.

THE SOUTHWEST

EL MÉDANO

$$$ **Playa Sur Tenerife**, tel. 922-176120, 922-176180, fax. 922-176337. On windsurfing beach, 70 rooms, restaurant, bar, pool, billiards, table tennis, library. Windsurfing boards can be rented next door (courses also provided).

$$ **El Médano**, Playa del Médano 2, tel. 922-177000, fax. 922-176048. Oldest hotel in El Médano, by the sea. Renovated rooms, not all with sea view; **Carel**, Avda. de los Príncipes 22, tel. 922-176066, fax. 922-176828. Simple boarding house on the way into the center, 20 rooms.

$ **Camping Nauta**, Cañada Blanca, near Las Gallettas, tel. 922-785118, 922-785027, fax. 922-795016. Small wooden bungalows, pool and sports facilities; also for caravans; open all year round.

Alabama's, between San Isidro and Granadilla, tel. 922-770608. Live music, American cooking. Popular with package tour groups, Sun-Thu 10 pm to midnight, Fri-Sat 10 pm to 2 am.

Plaza del Príncipe, tel. 922-176002, Mon-Fri 10 am to 1 pm (in peak season also 4 to 7 pm), Sat 9 am to 2 pm.

LAS GALLETAS

GOLF: **Amarillo Golf Country Club**, near Costa del Silencio, tel. 922-730295; **Golf del Sur**, between Las Galletas and Los Abrigos, tel. 922-731070, fax. 922-785272. 27-hole course; **Los Palos**, on the Carretera near Guaza, tel. 922-730080, fax. 922-731898. 9-hole course and golfing school.

GO-CARTS: **Karting Club Tenerife**, between Guaza & Las Chafiras, tel. 922-730703, daily from 10 am.

DIVING: Courses and excursions at **Buceo Tenerife Diving Center**, Calle María del Carmen García 22, tel. 922-731015; **Island Divers**, Urbanización Tamaide J42, Costa del Silencio, tel./fax. 922-730815.
Centro Médico, Calle Galván Bello 23, tel. 922-785092.
POST OFFICE: Calle Luís A. Cruz.
Entrada al Muelle, tel. 922-730133, Mon-Fri morn.

LOS ABRIGOS

SEAFOOD RESTAURANTS: **Perlas del Mar**, tel. 922-176414. Situated on a rocky outcrop on the eastern edge of the harbor; **La Langostera**, tel. 922-176319; **Vista Mar**, tel. 922-176156; **La Dorada**, tel. 922-176584, delicious paella; **Colibrí**, Las Galletas, Paseo Marítimo 9, tel. 922-730205. Terrace with sea view, fresh fish daily.

LOS CRISTIANOS

$$$ **Gran Hotel Arona**, Avda. de los Cristianos, tel. 922-750678, fax. 922-750243. At the end of the beach promenade, view of bay and harbor, restaurants and bars, pools, sauna, squash, fitness center; **Oasis Moreque**, Avda. Penetración, tel. 922-790366, fax. 922-792260. On the beach promenade, 170 rooms, swimming pool, tennis courts, playground.
Casa del Mar, Explanada del Muelle, tel. 922-793275 and 922-791323. Good seafood restaurant, awarded the Spanish Gastronomy Gold Medal in 1994 and 1995, Tue-Sun 1 to 11:30 pm; **El Cine**, Calle Juan Boriajo 8, tel. 909-044804. Small tapas bar with tables outside, Tue-Sun 7 am to 10:30 pm.
Parque Ecológico Las Águilas del Teide, on the road from Los Cristianos to Arona, tel. 922-753001, fax. 922-753062. Artistically arranged tropical landscape with kangaroos, crocodiles, hippopotami and penguins, parrot shows on open-air stage, restaurant. Flight displays with birds of prey, daily 9 am to 9 pm, variety performances in the evenings; **Centro Alfarero**, Arguayo, tel. 922-863485. Pottery museum, Tue-Sun 10 am to 1 pm and 4 to 7 pm, admission free.
Pirámide de Arona, Avda. de Las Américas, tel. 922-796360. Shows daily.
DISCOS: **El Templo**, north of the Autopista del Sur near Los Cristianos. Ancient Egyptian decor, dancing for young and old, daily 10:30 pm to 6 am.
PARASAILING: For info tel. 922-793824 or ask at the kiosk at the dry dock (Los Cristianos harbor).
WHALE AND DOLPHIN SPOTTING / DEEP SEA FISHING: See Los Gigantes / Puerto de Santiago.
Librería Barbara, Calle Generalísimo Franco/Juan Pablo Abril, tel./fax. 922-792301. From hiking maps to beach books (in various languages).

Centro Médico del Sur, Avda. de los Cristianos, tel. 922-790486.
POST OFFICE: Calle Los Sabandeños.
Centro Cultural, Calle General Franco, tel. 922-752492, Mon-Fri 9 am to 1 pm.

LOS GIGANTES / PUERTO DE SANTIAGO

$$$ **Los Gigantes**, Flor de Pascua 12, tel. 922-101020, fax. 922-100475. 225 rooms with balcony, bath, pool, sauna, tennis, squash, fitness center.
$$ **Barceló Santiago**, Puerto Santiago, Calle La Hondura, tel. 922-860912/925, fax. 922-861808 and 922-863036. Comfortable. Pools, sauna, massage, tennis, squash.
DIVING: **Baracuda Tauch Club** Heinz Scheffler, Paraíso Floral Hotel, tel. 922-740726, tel./fax. 922-741881; **San Borondon** Dan Mihajlivic, Playa San Juan, Marina 10, tel. 922-865614, fax. 922-865100; **Los Gigantes Diving Center** John Punton, Puerto de los Gigantes, P41, tel./fax. 922-860431.
WHALE AND DOLPHIN SPOTTING / DEEP SEA FISHING: Several places do this in the harbors of Los Cristianos, Playa San Juan, Los Gigantes and in the Puerto Colón of Las Américas.
Medical Center, Puerto Santiago, Calle Manuel Ravelo, tel. 922-861462.
POST OFFICE: Puerto de Santiago, Carretera General.
Avenida Marítima (behind the beach of La Arena), tel. 922-860348, Mon-Fri 9 am to 1 pm.

PLAYA DE LAS AMÉRICAS

$$$ **Gran Hotel Bahia del Duque**, tel. 922-713000, fax. 922-746916. Luxury first-class hotel by the sea, 362 rooms in several different buildings (some resembling historic structures on the island). Conference rooms, restaurants, bars, pools, tennis, squash, putting green, fitness center; **Jardín Tropical**, on the beach promenade, tel. 922-750100, fax. 922-752844. Quiet, luxurious, excellent restaurants, pool by the sea.
Las Rocas, hotel restaurant in the *Jardín Tropical*, Urbanización San Eugenio, tel. 922-750100. Terrace by the sea with a South Seas touch; fish, seafood, paella; **El Patio**, Hotel restaurant in the *Jardín Tropical*, tel. see *Las Rocas*. Has been awarded several prizes; **Harley's American Restaurant**, behind the Puerto Colón, Club Flamingo, tel. 922-796260. American style, cocktails, Mexican snacks, vegetarian food, open daily; **Otelo**, at entrance to the Barranco del Infierno, tel. 922-780374. Delicious Canarian cuisine, view of Adeje, Wed-Mon noon to 4 pm and 6 to 10 pm; **El Pescador de Alcalá**, harbor of Alcalá, tel. 922-865080.

Big fish restaurant; moderate prices; Wed-Mon noon to 3:30 pm and 7 to 11 pm; **Pancho**, Puerto Santiago, behind Playa de la Arena, tel. 922-101323. Specialties: fresh fish, pigeon in Malvasia wine. Large terrace, closed Mon; **Dieta Mediterránea**, at yacht harbor of Los Gigantes, Poblado Marinero 4, tel. 922-101134. Italian food, homemade pasta and good pizza, Tue-Sun 12:30 to 3:30 pm and 6:30 to 10:30 pm.

Verónica 1, **2** and **3**. Several discos for young people, latest hits; **Prisma's**, Avda. Litoral, international pop music, daily from midnight; **Macarena**, to the north of the Barranco del Rey. Music for the 25-45 age group, daily 10 pm to 5 am.

Casino, under the *Hotel Gran Tinerfe*, tel. 922-793712. Roulette, blackjack, slot machines. Identification required for the casino, admission to the machine hall is free.

HIKING: **Timah**, Adeje, Calle Tinerfe el Grande 1, tel. 922-710421 and 922-710242, fax. 922-710708. Helmuth Scheiber organizes mountain hiking groups for hikes on Tenerife and also other islands in the archipelago.

DIVING: **Gruber's Diving Center** Petra and Kurt Gruber, Park Club Europe, tel. 922-752708, fax. 922-796424, office hours daily 9:30 am to 6 pm. More offers in the Puerto Colón.

WHALE AND DOLPHIN SPOTTING / DEEP SEA FISHING: See Los Gigantes / Playa de Santiago.

WATER PARK: **Aguapark Octopus**, Playa de Las Américas, San Eugenio, Exit 29 on the Autopista del Sur, tel. 922-792266. Fun waterpark with plenty of pools and slides, daily 10 am to 6 pm.

Kiosko Artenerife, Avda. Litoral to the north of Las Verónicas. Canarian crafts, Mon-Sat 9:30 am to 2 pm and 3 to 7:30 pm; **Flea Market**, every evening on the Barranco del Rey, Thu and Sat mornings above the beach of Torviscas.

Salus Medical Center, Calle Panamá 3, tel. 922-796161.

POST OFFICE: Pueblo Canario.

Plaza del City Center, tel. 922-797668, Mon-Fri 9 am to 1 pm.

THE NORTH

BAJAMAR

$$ **Delfin**, Avda. del Sol, tel./fax. 922-540200. 66 rooms, mostly with balcony, restaurant, pool, tennis; **Neptuno**, Carretera General, tel. 922-542562, fax. 922-150402. Inexpensive.

Café Melita, Carretera General Punta del Hidalgo 171, tel. 922-540814. Terrace café, good filter coffee, cakes. Daily 9 am to 9:30 pm; **Olga**, Roque de las Bodegas, tel. 922-590220. Good rice and fish dishes, medium price category. Daily 11 am to 9 pm.

POST OFFICE: Calle Castillo.

GARACHICO

$$$ **Hotel San Roque**, C. Esteban de Ponte 32, tel. 922-133435, fax. 922-133406. In restored manor house (18th century), designer furniture and objets d'art in every room. 20 double rooms and apartments. Restaurant, sauna, heated pool.

$ **Il Giardino di Garachico**, Calle Esteban Ponte 8, tel./fax. 922-830245. Centrally located boarding house in the Canarian style with up to 20 beds.

Further accommodation possibilities in unrented **private apartments** are available at the sea promenade.

Il Giardino, Calle Esteban de Ponte 8, tel. 922-830245. Pizza and pasta on the patio of a Canarian house, moderate prices, closed Thu; **Rivamar**, between Los Silos and Garachico, Carretera General, tel. 922-831311. Fresh fish, seafood, meat à la canarienne, closed Tue; **Monteverde**, east of El Tanque on the Carretera General 2, tel. 922-830902. Simple Canarian restaurant, poultry, fresh fish, moderate prices, closed Mon.

Museo de Arte, Plaza de Santo Domingo, tel. 922-830000. Modern canarian art in the side-chapels of a monastery church. Mon-Sat 9 am to 1 pm; **Casa de Cultura**, Gloriéta de San Francisco. Art exhibitions, photos and documents relating to municipal history, stuffed marine animals, birds, butterflies and religious artefacts, Mon-Sat 9 am to 6 pm, Sun 9 am to 1 pm; **Castillo de San Miguel**. Exhibition of minerals, fossils, mussels and snails. Daily 9 am to 6 pm.

CAMEL RIDES: **Camello Center**, southwest of El Tanque, Carretera General, tel. 922-831191 and 922-133393.

DIVING: **Argonautes**, Calle Esteban Ponte 8, tel./fax. 922-830245.

SOUVENIRS: **Patio El Limonero**, directly opposite the Castillo de San Miguel. Also local crafts, Tue-Sat 10 amto 6 pm, Sun 10 am to 3 pm; **La Paredita**, El Tanque, tel. 922-136033. Studio of the painter Antoine Manfredi, paintings and sculptures.

POST OFFICE: Calle Martín de Andujar 1.

ICOD DE LOS VINOS

Carmen, Calle Hércules 2, tel. 922-810631. At the *Drago Milenario*, Canarian specialties, closed Sun evening and Mon from afternoon onwards.

Iglesia San Marcos. Liturgical equipment, religious raiment and a large filigree silver cross, mornings until 12:30; **El Mariposario del Drago**, tel. 922-815167. Exotic butterflies from all over the world in the glass-covered butterfly garden beneath the famous dragon tree, daily 9:30 am to 6 pm; **Biblioteca Expresión Contemporanea Antonín Artaud**, San Juan de la Rambla, Calle Estrecha 5, tel. 922-350484, fax. 922-350376. Artists' meeting place, library, studio, exhibition rooms, Thu 5 to 9 pm, Sat-Sun 10 am to 2 pm and 3 to 9 pm.

SOUVENIRS: **Arte Ycodem**, Calle Sebastían 4. Crafts (textiles, ceramics, souvenirs), Canarian wine. *WINE:* **Salón Canario del Vino**, Plaza de la Pila 5. Wine-tasting center with sales of Canarian wine, liqueurs and cheeses.

POST OFFICE: Calle de San Sebastián 11.

LA OROTAVA

$$$ **Hotel Victoria**, Calle Hermano Apolinar 8, tel. 922-331683, fax. 922-320519. Splendid interior design, 13 double rooms and a suite inside a 300-year-old renovated manor house in the heart of the Old Town. Terrace with view of the Old Town, Orotava Valley and Teide. Good Canarian restaurant.

$ **Silene**, Calle Tómas Zerolo 9, tel. 922-330199. Simple boarding house, three rooms.

Hijuela, Calle Tomás Pérez 1, part of the botanical gardens of Puerto de la Cruz; Mon-Sat 9 am to 2 pm; **Museo de Artesanía Iberoamericana**, Calle Tomás Zerolo 34, tel. 922-323376, fax. 922-335811. Musical instruments, ceramics, basket weaving, textiles, award-winning furniture, Mon-Fri 9 am to 6 pm, Sat 9 am to 2 pm; **El Pueblo Guanche – Museo Etnográfico**, Carrera del Escultor Estévez 17, tel. 922-322725, fax. 922-333488. Finds from the pre-Hispanic era. Kitchen from the former house is in original condition. The *Sabor Canario* restaurant has good Canarian cuisine, Mon-Sat 9:30 am to 7:30 pm (museum), restaurant open until late.

CRAFTS: **Casa Torrehermosa**, Calle Tomás Zerolo 27, tel. 922-304013. Products from the province of Santa Cruz de Tenerife in a renovated historic building dating from the 16th century, Mon-Fri 9:30 am to 6:30 pm, Sat 9:30 am to 2 pm; **Casa de los Balcones**, Calle San Francisco 3, tel. 922-330629. Calado embroidery and traditional work, in a historic building; **Casa del Turista** (also: **de la Alfombra**), opposite the Casa de los Balcones. In a historic building.

POST OFFICE: Plaza Patricio García.

Carrera del Escultor Estévez 2, tel. 922-323041.

LOS REALEJOS

$$$ **Maritim**, El Burgado 1, tel. 922-379000, fax. 922-379037. On the coast to the west of Puerto de la Cruz, 450 rooms, small botanical garden, baths, sports facilities; **Tierra de Oro**, Realejo Alto, tel. 922-341000 and 922-341213, fax. 922-344318. Spa hotel with 80 beds, German-run. Healthy food, fitness center, sauna, mineral water pool and outdoor swimming pool. Topless sunbathing terrace with view of the Orotava Valley. Can only be booked directly.

Gaiatours, Calle San Agustín 48, tel./fax. 922-355272. Tours of the Patronato de Turismo, including transportation, insurance and guides.

DIVING: **Atlantik**, to the west of Puerto de la Cruz, El Burgado 1, tel. 922-362801, fax. 922-344501. Hotel Maritim (behind the swimming pool), office hours: Mon-Fri 9 to 9:30 am, 12 to 1 and 5 to 5:30 pm, Sat 12:30 to 1 pm.

MASCA

$ The **El Guanche** restaurant, tel. 922-863424, organizes simple accommodation, half-board possible.

La Pimentera, tel. 922-863438. Quiet, with terrace, panoramic view. Good international cooking with Canarian touch, Wed-Mon 12 to 6 pm; **Casa Enrique – Chez Arlette**, tel. 922-863459. Surrounded by luxuriant foliage. Specialty: grilled lamb. Sun-Fri 11:30 am to 6:30 pm; **El Guanche**, tel. 922-863424. In a former village school, leafy terraces, Canarian-inspired cooking, daily 11 am to 6 pm.

PUERTO DE LA CRUZ

$$$ **Semiramis**, La Paz, Calle L. Cólogan Zulueta 27, tel. 922-373200, fax. 922-373193. All rooms with balcony. Garden, heated pools; **Tigaiga**, Parque del Taoro 28, tel. 922-383500, fax. 922-384055. In a palm park near the *Taoro* casino, restaurant, pool, tennis; **Marquesa**, C. Quintana 11, tel. 922-383151, fax. 922-386950. Historic building in the center, 92 rooms with bath, most with balcony. Pool, bars, good restaurant with terrace above pedestrian precinct.

$$ **Finca Ventoso**, Las Dehesas 73, tel./fax. 922-383820. Apartments for self-caterers, in a banana plantation.

$ **Los Geranios**, Ortsteil La Ranilla, Lomo 14, tel. 922-382810. Quiet boarding house in the harbor quarter with 10 rooms.

Magnolia, Avda. Marqués Villanueva del Prado 5, tel. 922-385614. Excellent restaurant for Catalan specialties. High prices; **Casa de Miranda**, Calle Santo Domingo 13, tel. 922-373871. In an 18th-century building. Comfortable atmosphere, good fish dishes, daily 1 to 11:30 pm; **Régulo**, Calle Pérez Zamora 16, tel. 922-384506. Fresh fish, international cuisine, Canarian dishes, Mon-Fri 12 to 3 pm and 6 to 11 pm; **El Monasterio**, above La Vera in La Montaña, Calle General de la Montaña, tel. 922-340707. In former monastery rooms. Specialty: meat grilled over charcoal, strong country wine, daily am to 1 pm; **Mi Vaca y Yo**, Calle Cruz Verde 3, tel. 922-385247 and 922-382086. Fish restaurant in the old fishing quarter, daily 1 to 3:30 pm and 7 to 11:30 pm.

Loro Parque, in the suburb of Punta Brava, tel. 922-374081 and 922-373841, fax. 922-375021. Biggest collection of parrots in the world. Shows with loros, sea lions and dolphins. Shark tunnel, bat caves, orchid house, daily 8:30 am to 5 pm; **Jardín de Aclimatación de La Orotava**, Calle Retama 2, tel. 922-383572. Botanical garden with many plants endemic to the Canaries, daily 9 am to 6 pm, in summer until 7 pm; **Bananera El Guanche**, 2 km east of Puerto, tel. 922-331853 and 922-330017. Plantation with video guide, sales of spirits and cut flowers. Free bus service from Playa Martiánez, daily 9 am to 6 pm; **Museo Arqueológico**, Calle del Lomo 9a, tel. 922-371465. Guanche pottery.

LIVE MUSIC: **Abaco**, El Durazno, Calle Casa Grande, tel. 922-370107. Nice cocktail bar in Canarian manor house (17th century), piano music (Thu-Sat after 10 pm) and chamber concerts, daily 8 pm to 2 am; **Bodega Mario's**, Calle Corales, tel. 922-375192. Basement restaurant with music from the Spanish mainland; **Otto's Piano Bar "Blue Note,"** Calle Zamora, 15. tel. 922-380943. Jazz cellar, Mon-Sat 10 pm to 3 am; **Andromeda**, Avda. Colón, tel. 922-383852 and 922-383899. Nightclub of the Lago Martiánez with Varieté and dancing, closed Mon.

CASINO: **Casino de Taoro**. Roulette, blackjack, slot machines. Minimum age 18, admission fee.

TENNIS: **Tennis Center Miramar**, La Romantica II (west of Puerto de la Cruz), Urbanización Valparaiso, Calle Los Tulipanes 2, tel. 922-340408, fax. 922-353046. Multilingual trainers, three courts. Badminton, swimming pool, bistro, sauna, qualified masseur.

Hiking with Gregorio: Apply for this in the Hotel *Tigaiga*, tel. 922-383500 (from 4 pm), fax. 922-330910. Organized tours with bus transfers. Internet: http://members.aol.com/gregorio2.

SOUVENIRS: **Karinia**, Calle Aceviño 45, tel. 922-371372. A woman designer creates blouses, jackets, pants, cloths, pictures and hiking clothing. Sat and Sun 10 am to 1 pm or by prior arrangement.

CRAFTS: **Artenerife**, Explanada del Muelle, tel. 922-388202. Kiosk at the harbor; **Casa Tafuriaste**, above Puerto de la Cruz, Carretera de la Luz – Las Candias 29, tel. 922-333396. Museum and ceramic shop in building dating from the 17th century, Mon-Sat 10 am to 6 pm, admission fee. *MUSIC:* Canarian music productions in all styles at **Manzanas** on Calle San Telmo. *FLEA MARKET:* Sat mornings, market building El Tejar, San Felipe district 9 am to 2 pm.

Ambulatorio, Calle El Pozo, tel. 922-372287.

POST OFFICE: Calle El Pozo (bus station).

Plaza de Europa, tel. 922-386000, Mon-Fri 9 am to 8 pm, Sat 9 am to 1 pm.

SANTA ÚRSULA

La Quinta Park, highway exit to the west of Santa Úrsula, La Quinta 21, tel. 922-300266, fax. 922-300513. 200 apartments and studios with balconies. Garden with pools, restaurant, bar, supermarket, tennis, squash, spa center with doctor, fitness center, cosmetic salon, hydrotherapy.

Los Corales, Calle Cuesta de la Villa 30, tel. 922-301918. Good international and Canarian dishes, Tue-Sun 12:30 to 4 pm and 7 to 11 pm; **Faisan Azul**, La Matanza, Calle Acentejo 68, tel. 922-577782. French and German cuisine.

TACORONTE

Camping Playa La Arena, Mesa del Mar, tel. 922-572555. Bungalows for two people.

Casa del Vino, country house in the *La Baranda* area with wine museum, tasting cellar, bar, restaurant, shop. Autopista del Norte, "El Sauzal" exit, tel. 922-572535/42 (museum), 922-563388 (restaurant), fax. 922-572744. Museum: Tue-Sat 11 am to 8 pm, Sun 11 am to 6 pm. Bar: 11 am to 10:30 pm. Restaurant: 1 to 4 pm and 7:30 to 10:30 pm; **Museo Etnográfico de Tenerife**, Carretera Tacoronte-Valle de Guerra 44, tel. 922-543053, fax. 922-544498. Farming implements in the De Carta country house (17th century); Tue-Sat 10 am to 5 pm, Sun 10 am to 2 pm.

WINE: **Bodegas Álvaro**, Tacoronte, Calle Waque 4, tel. 922-572331, closed Sun.

POST OFFICE: Punta del Hidalgo, Carretera General 128.

THE TWO METROPOLISES

LA LAGUNA

$$ **Aguere**, Calle Obispo Rey Redondo 55, tel. 922-259490, fax. 922-631633. Has seen batter days. 22 rooms in an 18th-century building, various conference rooms, large lobby, boutiques; **Nivaria**, Plaza del Adelantado 11, tel. 922-264298, fax. 922-259634. Best hotel in La Laguna, mainly apartments. Café bar, salon, squash.

Tasca Lagunera, Plaza Doctor Juan Régulo Pérez 6, tel. 922-256653. Elegant and busy restaurant, good wine list; **La Gotera**, Calle San Agustín 9, tel. 922-255666. Comfortable, in the Old Town, medium price category, Mon-Sat 1 to 4 pm and 8 pm to 2 am; **Los Limoneros**, expensive restaurant for big city people in

Los Naranjeros, tel. 922-636637 and 922-636144, closed Sun.

Museo de Historia de Tenerife, Calle San Agustín 22, tel. 922-630103 and 922-630121. Museum in the Casa Lercano (built 1593) documenting history of the island in Spanish times, Tue-Sat 10 am to 5 pm, Sun 10 am to 2 pm; **Museo de la Ciencia y el Cosmos**, road from Santa Cruz to La Laguna (via La Cuesta), Via Lactea, tel. 922-263454/494. Modern interactive museum, planetarium and film room, Tue-Sun 10 am to 8 pm; **Casa de los Capitanes**, Calle Obispo Rey Redondo 5. Exhibitions on the cultural history of the Canary Islands, Mon 5 to 8 pm, Tue-Sat 11 am to 1 pm and 5 to 8 pm, Sun 11 am to 1 pm; **Ermita San Miguel**, Plaza del Adelantado. Modern art, Mon 5 to 8 pm, Tue-Sat 11 am to 1 pm and 5 to 8 pm, Sun 11 am to 1 pm.

El Tocuyo, Calle Juan de Viana. Wine bar.

DISCOS: **O'Clock Disco Pub**, Calle Barcelona 6, tel. 922-633561, bar opens at 7 pm, then a DJ or live band; **Discoteca NOOCTUA**, near the airport, "Los Rodeos" exit northbound, Fri and Sat from 11:30 pm.

PUBS: On weekends the action starts from midnight onwards, e.g., in the **Nueva Visión** (C. Elias Serra Rafols) with its video wall, in the **Bar de Blues** (C. Doctor Zamenhof 9; occasional live music or poetry readings), and in the **Buho Jazz Bar** (Calle Catedral 3).

Main shopping street in La Laguna: *Calle Obispo Rey Redondo* (fashion and shoe stores). *BOOKS:* **Lemus**, Calle Heraclio Sánchez 64, tel. 922-253244. *MARKETS:* **Mercado** on the Plaza del Adelantado; also with biological and herbal stalls.

WINE: **La Vinoteca**, Plaza de la Concepción 24, tel. 922-261602. Spanish and Canarian wines.

GOLF: **Campo de Golf**, Los Rodeos, tel. 922-630115. Signposted on the Autopista del Norte at the "Los Rodeos" exit. 18 holes.

Hospital Universitario de Canarias, Carretera Cuesta-Taco, tel. 922-678000.

POST OFFICE: Calle Santo Domingo.

Pavilion on the Plaza del Adelantado.

SANTA CRUZ DE TENERIFE

AECAN, Calle Villalba Hervás 4, tel. 922-240816, fax. 922-244003. Agency with "turismo rural" program, renovated country houses on Tenerife, La Palma, La Gomera and El Hierro.

$$$ **Mencey**, Calle Dr. José Naveiras 38, tel. 922-276700, fax. 922-280017. For VIPs and the jet set, 300 rooms and suites, elegant restaurant, bar, gardens.

$$ **Atlántico**, Calle del Castillo 12, tel. 922-246375, fax. 922-246378. In the pedestrian precinct, 60 rooms; **Horizonte**, Calle Santa Rosa de Lima 11, tel. 922-275359. In the town center, 45 small rooms; **Plaza**, Plaza de la Candelaria 10, tel. 922-272453, fax. 922-275160. Centrally located, bar on the rooftop terrace.

$ **Mova**, Calle San Martín 33, tel. 922-283261. Family-run boarding house in town center, 20 small rooms.

SEAFOOD RESTAURANTS IN SAN ANDRÉS (all by the sea with the exception of Pinchitos): **El Rubí**, tel. 922-549673, rice specialties; **Ramón**, tel. 922549308. Specialty: perch in red fish sauce; **La Costera**, tel. 922549006, closed Sun evenings; **Los Pinchitos**, Calle Guillén 14, tel. 922-549283. Good grilled fish. *OTHER RESTAURANTS:* **Los Menceyes**, elegant restaurant in the Hotel Mencey; **Café del Príncipe**, Plaza del Príncipe, tel. 922-278810. Fish, Canarian cuisine, medium prices, closed Mon; **Cervecería Central**, Calle La Luna/San Clemente, tel. 922-291114. Tapas, Canarian dishes, tables also out of doors, daily 8 am to 2 am; **Montecarlo**, Avda. de Anaga 43, tel. 922-289841. On the harbor promenade. French-influenced cuisine, closed Sun; **Harley's**, Calle Mendez Nuñez 5, tel. 922-293000. Mexican, Italian and Asian dishes, video wall and bowling alley, daily noon to midnight.

Museo de la Naturaleza y el Hombre, Calle Fuente Morales, tel. 922-209314-5. Double museum in former hospital, archeological and natural history department, Tue-Sun 10 am to 8 pm; **Museo Municipal**, Calle José Murphy 4, tel. 922-244358. Municipal art gallery, in summer Mon-Fri 10 am to 1:30 pm and 12:30 to 6:30 pm, winter Mon-Fri 10 am to 8 pm, admission free; **Centro de Fotografía**, Plaza Isla de la Madera, tel. 922-290735. Alternating exhibition of photographs and paintings, Tue-Sat 10 am to 1 pm and 5 to 8 pm, Sun 11 am to 1 pm, admission free.

Teatro Guimerá, large theater for plays, opera, ballet, concerts and festival events.

DISCOS: **KU**, Santa Cruz, La Granja Park, Avda. Madrid, tel. 922-203636. Shows and good Mexican restaurant; **Ñoh!**, Santa Cruz, Avda. de Anaga 32, tel. 922281453. Trendy cocktail bar with tables out on the boulevard and a dance floor, daily 10:30 pm to 3 am.

PUBS: Around the Plaza de la Paz and on the Avenida de Anaga. *TRENDY BARS:* **Parra**, Pasaje Sitja 19; **El Desván**, Pasaje Sitja 17. Sometimes with live music at weekends.

Long Way, Calle Castillo 41, office 221, tel./fax. 922-292061. Also mountain-biking, paragliding and diving; **Canarias Trekking**, Calle Quevedo 4, Edifício Gran Vía, intermediate floor, office 2, tel./fax. 922-201051. Tour organization.

BINGO: Hall for 400 players on Calle Imeldo Serís.

Main shopping streets in Santa Cruz: *Calle del Castillo* with fashion boutiques, drugstores and electronic stores and *Calle Béthencourt Alfonso.* More expensive boutiques between *Calle del Castillo* and *Calle* del Pilar *Señora de África*, daily market in the mornings, flea market on Sun.

DIPLOMATIC REPRESENTATION: British Consulate: Plaza de Weyler, Santa Cruz de Tenerife, tel. 922-286863 (if you phone outside of office hours a recording will give you a number), Mon-Fri 9 am to noon.
American Embassy: Call Cerrano 75, 28006 Madrid, tel. 091-5774000, Mon-Fri 10 am to noon.

POST OFFICE: Plaza de España.

Plaza de España (in the Palacio Insular), tel. 922-239592 and 922-239500, fax. 922-605781, daily 8 am to 6 pm.

THE SOUTH AND THE CENTER

ARONA / LA ESCALONA

$$ **Tenerife Tracks & Trails**, La Escalona, Mountain Lodge, Los Quemados 2, tel. 922-725358. Apartments for self-caterers and hikers in rural environment. Guided group tours and hikes (English and Spanish; from 8 participants up). Bar, pool, billiards, table tennis and darts.

Patio Canario, Arona, Calle Domínguez Alfonso 4, tel. 922-725503. Belgian and Canarian cuisine. Reservation recommended, Tue-Sat 1 to 3 pm and 7 to 11 pm (winter; 8 to 11 pm in summer); **El Refugio**, near Arona, El Topo 34 (access signposted), tel. 922-725894. International cuisine, Tue-Thu 12 to 9 pm, Thu from 6 pm.

Tenerife Tracks & Trails (see "Accommodation").

CANDELARIA

$$ **Tenerife Tour**, Caletillas district, Avda. Generalísimo 170, tel. 922-500200/4, fax. 922-502363. 90 rooms in bungalow style by the sea, garden, pools, tennis, boules, conference rooms, disco.

Basilica, consecrated to the patron saint of the Canary Islands, daily 7:30 am to 1 pm and 3 to 7:30 pm.

Centro Médico de Candelaria, Calle José Antonio near the harbor.

POST OFFICE: Calle José Antonio.

Centro de Información Turística: Caletillas, Plaza de la Constitución.

GÜIMAR

La Cuevita de Nemesio, Arafo, Carretera La Cumbre near km 2, tel. 922-513402. Cave restaurant with Canarian cuisine, delicious specialties. Wed-Mon 1 pm to midnight.

Parque Etnográfico Pirámides de Güimar, Calle Chacona, tel. 922-514510, fax. 922-514511. With Museo Casa Charcona. Internet: http://www.fredolsen.es/piramides.

LA ESPERANZA

Las Cañadas, Carretera General 73 (access road to the Cañadas), tel. 922-548030. Large dining room, bar, café and souvenir shop. Specialties: rabbit, suckling pig and chicken baked in a wood oven.

TEIDE

$$ **Parador de Turismo Las Cañadas del Teide**, tel. 922-386415, fax. 922-382352. Located 2,100 meters above sea level, pool, sauna, fitness center, restaurant, small museum.

$ **Refugio de Altavista**, mountain hut 3,300 meters up, limited to 50 people, apply by phone at tel. 922-239811 or 922-239592.

Group accommodation in log cabins: In the Teide National Park near Arenas Negras. Information from the Ayuntamiento de Garachico, Plaza de la Libertad 1, E-38450 Garachico, tel. 922-830000/01, fax. 922-831301.

TEIDE CABLE CARS: As far as the Rambleta (3,550 meters). No service if windy, and long waiting times in peak season, daily 9 am to 4 pm, tel. 922-287837.

Hiking information from the Centro de Visitantes.

Centro de Visitantes: Information center about Teide National Park near El Portillo. Bookstore, video show, various signboards and maps; **Patronato del Parque Nacional de las Cañadas del Teide**, Santa Cruz, Calle Emilio Calzadilla 5, tel. 922-290129. This is where you can get permission to ascend the summit. Guided hikes through the Cañadas, daily 9 am to 4 pm.

VILAFLOR

$ **Alta Montaña**, Morro del Cano 1, tel. 922-709049, fax. 922-709000. Quiet, 25 beds, ideal for hikers. Rooms with bath and terrace, pool, healthy food. Double room with breakfast 6,000 Ptas.

El Mirador, panoramic view of Vilaflor. Tel. 922-709135; Mon-Thu 10 am to 8 pm, Sat, Sun 12 to 8 pm.

Parque San Roque, tel. 922-709124. Adventure park with museum, goat enclosure, Mexican hacienda, souvenir shop with restaurant, daily 10 am to 6 pm (museum) and 11 am to 10 pm (restaurant).

Rosetas and *Calados*: In the store on Calle Hermano Pedro 28 and in the *Multivision Parque Nacional del Teide* outside town in the direction of Arona, Camino Lomo Oreja 6. You can also get other craft items here, plus honey, rum, mojo and gofio.

VILLA DE ARICO

$$ **Aricotour**, Carretera General 11, tel./fax. 922-161133. Organizes accommodation in old farmhouses, info about hikes, visits to dairies, etc.

papelera

DIGA
Sports

THE SENDERO TURÍSTICO

Many a vacationer has come to the conclusion at the end of a trip to Tenerife: "We should bring our hiking equipment along next time." Beaches, water sports and cultural points of interest are highly praised in travel brochures, however, there is relatively little said about the opportunities for hiking on the island – even though the conditions for exploring Tenerife on foot are absolutely ideal. Up to the medium elevations there is a pleasant climate with hardly any sudden changes in the weather, as there often is in the Alps, for instance. Numerous hiking trails lead through a unique and for the most part unspoiled landscape. And, last but by no means least, Mount Teide, at 3,717 meters the highest mountain in Spain, presents an attractive and challenging destination for hikers.

For easy hiking tours on Tenerife no special equipment is required. Comfortable clothing, good hiking boots, a small backpack for food and drinks, a hat for protection against the sun, and a sweater or jacket will be all you should need. Before setting out on longer hikes, a few half-day excursions should help you to familiarize yourself with conditions on the island. Orientation is aided by *Sendero Turístico* (Touristic Path) signs at the starting points of trails.

Barranco del Infierno

Some of the best hiking is the half-day trip through "Hell's Ravine," the *Barranco del Infierno*, however, you may find it pretty crowded on weekends. The trail leads alongside a brook and passes through three distinct vegetational zones along its four-kilometer length. Here you can see a variety of plants only found on the Canary Islands.

The starting point for this hike is the ancient town of Adeje, which is 30 minutes by car or bus from Playa de Las Américas. Turn to the left at the parish church of Santa Ursula until you reach the Casa Fuerte, a former earl's residence. On your right-hand side a steep road leads up to the entrance of the barranco, which is signposted. Here enormous euphorbias and prickly pears grow beneath the steep rock faces. The deeper you penetrate into "Hell's Ravine," the denser the vegetation gets. In spring, the Canarian bellflower, with its distinctive large orange blossoms, can be seen here. At the end of the ravine there is a mossy rock face, down which the water runs in myriad rivulets. As the trail ends here, you'll have to take the same way back to the starting point.

Paisaje Lunar

A little bit more off the beaten track, and a wonderful alternative for first-time visitors to Tenerife, is a second popular trail for hikers. You can find it not far from Adeje near Vilaflor, the highest village on the island. For access, however, you'll need your own car. Follow the road from Vilaflor in the direction of the Cañada National Park.

Just above the village, a dirt track leads to the right, which is signposted "Lomo Blanco / Paisaje Lunar." After about seven kilometers you'll come to a signpost marked "Paisaje Lunar." This is the start of a two-hour hike through a bizarre landscape full of light and dark pillars of calcareous tufa, one beside the other, which have been formed by the wind. They have given the region its name: *Paisaje Lunar* (Lunar Landscape). Keep in mind that the sun's rays are extremely strong in this barren region; it is recommended that you wear a long-sleeved shirt as well as a hat.

Previous pages: On the Playa de las Teresitas. Taking a break during a mountain-bike tour in Masca. Right: Euphorbia, a species of succulent endemic to Tenerife.

Masca

An hour's drive north of Playa de Las Américas is the hamlet of Masca. Having remained largely untouched by tourism for quite a long time, it has kept much of its original charm. If you plan a hike in this region, you should allow some time for a stroll around the town, through the picturesque lanes with houses displaying the architecture that is typical of the Canary Islands.

The first hike starting out from Masca leads through the La Tabaiba pass, through the Teno Mountains, and into the small town of Buenavista del Norte. The 11-kilometer hike takes about three to four hours. Regular buses run from the end point of the hike back to Masca (remember to have a look at bus schedules in Masca before you set off). The marked trail runs in the same direction as the road connecting the two villages, however, you will be hiking on old trails that are set back some distance from the road.

From the few houses of Casas La Vica, a short distance behind Masca, a trail beside the road to your right leads up to the pass, through terraced fields, before descending, now to the left of the road, much more gently into the high valley of El Palmar. Cactus fields alternate with cultivable terraces, vineyards and banana fields, and trees bearing citrus and other tropical fruits. Buena Vista, the destination of our ramble, can already be seen from afar.

Breathtakingly beautiful, but not all that easy to hike, is the trail from Masca down through a deep ravine to the sea. Particularly after heavy rainfalls, the trail can be extremely slippery in some places. Moreover, there is a danger of falling rocks. It is best if you undertake this hike with a partner, or else as part of a guided tour. The latter option offers an advantage, in that participants are picked up on the coast by a cutter and taken back to Los Gigantes, thus saving the three-hour return journey. The route starts in the lower part of Masca, the starting point is well

signposted. After that follow the brook through the *barranco* down to the sea. The hike down the winding path into the ravine is one of the most rewarding you can take on Tenerife.

The Anaga Mountains

The northeastern part of Tenerife is dominated by the Anaga mountain range. Due to the climatic conditions of the Canary Islands, the trade winds bring dense clouds into this mountainous region. Although it seldom rains here, the air is constantly humid. As a consequence, there is rich and varied vegetation in the Anaga Mountains all year round.

Off the winding mountain road from La Laguna to Chamorga there are interesting hiking trails through a wood with Canadian pines. The views of the dramatic rock faces of the steep coast are spectacular from here. The respective starting points are marked with wooden signposts ("Sendero Turístico"). A simple map of trails in the Anaga range is available in all tourist offices.

A particularly rewarding sight in the Anaga Mountains is the remote cave village of Chamorga on the western side of the range. It is accessible by two hiking trails: if you are starting from the coast, you set out from Punta del Hidalgo; if you're already in the mountains, the small village of Las Carboneras serves as the starting point. Only if you're fairly surefooted and do not suffer from vertigo should you attempt the well-signposted hike from Punta de Hidalgo, for the narrow path runs just along the edge of the precipitous rocky coast in places.

From Las Carboneras, which is situated a few kilometers below the ridge, the path is somewhat easier to manage, in spite of a steep ascent at the beginning. In both cases, however, the cave village will be reached after about a two-hour walk. Chamorga itself is the starting point for an extremely varied, one-day circular route around the northeastern tip of the island via El Draguillo, Las Palmas and Roque Bermejo.

Mount Teide

The highlight of any hiking holiday on Tenerife is without a doubt the ascent of Mount Teide. The peak of the highest Spanish mountain proudly rises to 3,717 meters above sea level. On very clear days you have a remarkable view from here of all the islands of the Canarian archipelago. Although the peak of Mount Teide rises markedly up above the tradewind clouds that are so common here, and the sun may be seen from about 1,800 meters all year round, you should be aware of the brisk temperatures at this height. An icy wind generally blows at the higher elevations, and in the winter months there is snow cover.

Above: Experiencing nature on a mountain hike. Right: Climbing the Guajara offers a magnificent few of Mount Teide.

If you plan to hike in this region, call in at the visitor center (*Centro de Visitantes*) which lies off the main road to the national park not far from El Portillo. From here guided tours are available free of charge.

There is a four to five hour hike that can be undertaken from the visitor center to the *Parador Las Canadas del Teide* hotel, which presents a good opportunity for trailblazers to get accustomed to conditions on Mount Teide. A signposted path leads gently up and down from the foot of Teide below the edge of the *caldera* through a volcanic landscape which seems to be rather monotonous at first impression. Only in the course of the hike will you begin to recognize the distinguishing colors and forms of the lava stone hereabouts, and to discover the various plants that are able to survive in this inhospitable region. Good hiking boots, strong sun protection and sufficient drinking water are absolutely indispensable on this hike. From the *parador* there are buses going back to the visitor center, where you can also inquire about the bus schedule.

The starting point for the climb to the mountain's peak is situated at an altitude of 2,360 meters, and near the 40.5-kilometer mark on the road between the *Centro de Visitantes* and the *parador.* The four to five hour hike does not require any special mountaineering ability, however, you should keep in mind that the mountain air gets thinner and thinner as you ascend, and thus puts a strain on your supply of oxygen to the blood.

At almost 3,300 meters the steep and winding trail leads past the newly renovated Altavista mountain hut that provides simple accomodation for hikers. If you get here in the evening, you can climb up to the summit in the first rays of daylight while the sun is rising. As the government has been restricting hiking for the past several years on the last 160 meters from the mountain stop of the cable railway, it would be a good idea to inquire at the visitor center about current regulations (tel. 922-290129).

CYCLING ON TENERIFE

First-time visitors to Tenerife will probably find cycling on the largest of the Canary Islands rather difficult: enormous differences in altitude and busy traffic in the towns and resort areas are not exactly conducive to relaxed and enjoyable cycling tours. Individual travelers having their own bike trasported by plane to the vacation island will experience their first shock at the airport: the first few kilometers have to be covered along the freeway.

The tourism trade has not yet adapted itself to the the increasing demand for bicycle routes, so that few designated cycling trails are available. The few competent bicycle rental companies are hidden in the jungle of the various entertainment districts packed with shops and restaurants, and are not that easy to spot. And yet, despite all this, Tenerife has a great many varied and attractive routes to offer cyclists thanks to the diversity of its landscape.

Riding High on Mount Teide

Teide National Park casts a spell on virtually every visitor to Tenerife. As many as four access roads lead to the remote high plateau lying at the foot of the highest mountain in Spain. In order to cover the elevation gain of more than two thousand meters from the coast, you'll have to put up with a queasy feeling in your stomach if you're traveling by bus or car, as the road up has innumerable twists and turns. The cyclist, on the other hand, will be dripping with sweat by the time he arrives at the top of the plateau. But once you have ridden your bike between the bizarre rock towers and alongside magnificent volcanic peaks, you will certainly never forget the fascination that cycling on Tenerife evokes.

The Teide National Park undoubtedly presents the ultimate challenge to cyclists. Racing, touring and mountain bikers alike will find the terrain here ideal for their own style of cycling. The asphalt road leading through the national park as well as the fine graveled paths leave scope for plenty of tours of exploration. The volcanic rock offers an enormous diversity of forms and colors, with broom and *taginaste* spreading a sweet fragrance between the lumps of rock, above all in early summer. High above the wreath of clouds caused by the trade winds, you actually feel an overwhelming sense of peace and freedom.

And yet it is not our intention to conceal the fact that that only hardy, well-trained and experienced cylicsts will take pleasure in the adventure called Teide. Cool winds, at times whirling up the dust, the mountain air that gets much thinner the higher you go, and the blinding rays of the sun have to be coped with. Moreover, dramatic drops and rises in temperature, depending on the time of the day, can be a real problem for some people. Keep in mind when starting out from the coast that you have to be as fit as a fiddle to make the ascent, and that there are hardly any opportunities to obtain refreshments along the way.

As an alternative to tackling the mountain on your own, Diga Sports in Playa de Las Américas (Park Club Europe Tenerife, Avda. Rafael Puig 26, tel. 922-793009, fax 922-176837) offers guided tours in the national park. You will be picked up and brought uphill by minibus; afterwards, you can start your trip from above Vilaflor, for example.

A Tour of the Island

You do not have to climb up the Teide plateau, however, to experience the island's full beauty. In the lower regions,

Right: This is the only way to travel – stopping off for some refreshment before tackling the next stage of the ride (the port of El Médano).

too, there are attractive routes, but good physical condition is always required. Island routes definitely suit the intermediate to advanced cyclist; due to the extreme differences in altitude and as some stretches of road are heavily traveled, there is no cycling simply for pleasure. If you're fit, however, you can easily cycle around the island in three or four days.

An ideal starting point for a round-trip ride is Adeje on the southwest coast. If you want to avoid the troublesome freeway when starting out from Playa de Las Américas, it is recommendable to cover the first few kilometers by bus or taxi. From Adeje the road leads down to the coast and then through the fishing villages of San Juán and Alcalá, straight to Los Gigantes. Already from afar you can see the rocky cliffs dropping steeply off above the natural harbor.

You can watch the world go by in one of the street cafés in the harbor and have a much deserved drink: you'll need it in view of the ascent yet to come, for you have to overcome an elevation gain of no less than 900 meters on an 11-kilometer road. The street winds its way in a multitude of hairpin turns via Tamaimo to Santiago del Teide.

Less busy, but also somewhat longer, is the route via Los Pajares, Chío and the pottery village of Arguayo. Behind Santiago del Teide there is a fertile, high valley that lies embedded between the rugged Teno massif and Mount Teide. In addition to cornfields, vineyards, and fig and almond trees are plentiful here.

The Teno range is situated in the far northwest of the island, its slopes dropping steeply off towards the coast. Not that long ago nothing but narrow trails led to this remote part of the island. Today the route to charming Masca, lying hidden above a gorge, is accessible via a narrow, winding tarred road.

There is another small ascent to the pass, from which there are fantastic views, before the village appears far below. A 12-kilometer downhill ride to Buenavista on the northern coast follows. In the center of the town some beautiful

17th and 18th century houses can be admired.

At the coast near Buenavista the first banana plantations appear. There are still several of them to come. Via Los Silos and Garachico you get to Icod de los Vinos, which attracts considerable crowds because it boasts the allegedly oldest and most beautiful dragon tree on the Canary Islands. The town actually acquired its fame, however, through wine production, which played a very significant role in its past.

Three kilometers after Icod de los Vinos you leave the busy coastal road and pedal on a by-road up in the direction of La Guancha. There are amazing views along the way of the increasingly steep cliffs. You cross ravines, including the Barranco de Rambla, which is overgrown with ferns and bushes. Soon there is a gorgeous view of the Valle de la Orotava. Just how densely populated the coast is can be seen by the numerous white houses. After Tarasca, a scenic downhill ride with numerous hairpin bends to Realejo Alto begins. When you arrive at the central plaza, keep going in the direction of La Montaneta, and head for the upper part of La Orotava via Cruz Santa and La Perdona.

Above: Mountain-bikers find the best terrain for their hobby in the Anaga Mountains.

La Orotava is one of the most beautiful towns on Tenerife; the Old Town, which is classified as a historical monument with its bustling Plaza de la Constitución, is worth a lengthy stop. Anyone who happens to come along on Corpus Christi Day will be welcomed by the sight of a colorful "carpet" of sand and fine earth, which is skillfully laid out on the occasion of the annual parade.

From here you head off along the north coast on busy Route 820 through the towns of Santa Ursula and La Victoria, until you come to a right turn in La Mantanza heading towards Agua García. This part of the ride is along a narrow road, which is quite steep in places. From here you keep pedaling uphill for another five kilometers before you arrive in the village of La Esperanza. Here you touch the very beginning of the Bosque de la Esperanza, a dense forest full of Canarian pines and eucalyptus trees. The trees obtain the moisture they need for their prolific growth from the trade-wind clouds which constantly drift towards the slopes of the mountain. Through this forest a charming route leads straight to the Teide National Park.

After this leg of your journey, we recommend that you avoid the capital Santa Cruz. It is true that the capital is worth a visit, but getting back out of the city by bike is a race with the devil. It is certainly much more pleasant to head for the eastern coast via El Tablero. The long descent slopes down to Route 822, which you can follow all the way to Los Cristianos.

You'll soon put distance between yourself and the coast with its freeway. Leading gently upwards all the time, the road leads to the basin of Güímar. Often dark trade-wind clouds cling to the mountain slopes hereabouts, although it seldom rains. Güímar has developed into a thriving agricultural center. Dry farming here facilitates up to four vegetable harvests a year.

The road to Granadilla (altitude 700 meters) is among the most beautiful stretches Tenerife has to offer cyclists, and covers a distance of approximately 50 kilometers. The road, which is only lightly traveled, leads through fascinating *barrancos* that may be crossed by ancient stone bridges. There are continuously magnificent views of the coast along this route. Even Santa Cruz is still visible from a distance. Before you arrive at Arico, more and more rock caves become apparent, where, it is said, the Guanches used to live. Before the final ascent to Granadilla you cross a canyon-like gorge, where reddish-colored rocks offer a delightful view.

The last stage of the trip from Granadilla is very easy. You coast downhill nearly all the way back into the sunny tourist center of the south. The highlights of the scenery on this enthralling descent are the Barranco de Orchilla and the Mirador de la Centinela observation platform, from which you enjoy an exhilarating view of the black Roque Imoque.

(Total distance of the round-trip ride: 220 kilometers. Adeje-Buenavista 52 kilometers; La Oratova 45 kilometers; Guímar 53 kilometers; Los Cristianos 70 kilometers.)

Detour into the Green Anaga Mountains

A rewarding one-day trip to the northeast of the island leads from La Laguna through parts of the wooded Anaga range. The lush vegetation is the result of above-average rainfall, caused by the impact of the trade winds when they collide with the mountains. Numerous bird species, ranging from the woodpecker to the Egyptian vulture, can be observed here.

For the first leg of the trip, head for the vantage point of Lomo Alto. If the weather is good, you may spot the summit of Mount Teide looming in front of you. Next, you'll find yourself cycling steadily along a ridge, climbing and descending from one overwhelming view to another. Occasionally you will plunge deep into the dark forest.

From the Mirador Pico del Inglés you can see a long way – even Gran Canaria comes into view on a clear day – so allow some time for this short diversion from the trail.

At the crossroads of El Bailadero, cyclists who are in good condition and still have the energy have the opportunity to carry on for another 20 kilometers to the remote mountain village of Chamorga and back; others can tackle the 11-kilometer descent to San Andrés at once. From there you ride along the coast straight to Santa Cruz.

(Total distance: 42 kilometers.)

WATER SPORTS

Windsurfing

Thanks to the trade winds blowing steadily from the northeast, the southeast coast is the most suitable for windsurfing purposes. Among the true "surfing freaks," El Médano is considered to be a prime spot for this activity. Here the wind and waves demand your best performance, particularly during the winter months. Small wonder, then, that there are numerous annual World Cup races in El Médano attracting not only surfers, but crowds of curious onlookers as well. Both the Surf Center Playa Sur at the south beach and the Station Blue Water in the Hotel Calimar Atlantic Playa cater specifically to the needs of surfers, and try to attract cultomers with windsurfing courses. Both have well-trained staff.

Beginners as well as those having reached a somewhat intermediate level will look for easier areas to surf. There are courses and equipment rentals on offer at the beaches of Los Cristianos, Playa de Las Américas and Las Teresitas. Here one can venture into the calmer waters protected from the strong winds and surf according to one's own ability.

Sailing

If you're sailing on a yacht or catamaran in the waters of the Canary Islands, you'll be able to drop anchor on any of Tenerife's coasts in one of the total of seven sports harbors the island has to offer. This includes those in Santa Cruz, Puerto de la Cruz, Güímar, Los Gigantes, Los Cristianos and Puerto de Colón.

Next to Los Gigantes, the Puerto de Colón is considered the center of sailing. Here old seadogs and captains-to-be meet each other to chew the fat about their hobby, as well as to see and be seen. The courses and charters on offer range from a trip on your own by catamaran to a two-hour- excursion with a skipper up to a US $300 week-long course. Don't forget you need a valid sailing certificate if you plan to go on tour on your own.

Right: The jagged rock formations on the seabed offer an ideal environment for creatures such as the moray eel.

Scuba Diving

Scuba diving can be especially rewarding in the Canary Islands. The volcanic rock continues underwater and drops off steeply in many places. Bizarre rock formations, caves, grottoes, archways and chimneys provide for interesting and varied dives. Visibility is generally quite good, but after a heavy rainfall it will often take a few days until the particles of soil which have been washed in by the rain settle on the seabed. In summer the water temperature is so high that even in depths of 20 meters a wet suit of two to five millimeters thickness is sufficient.

The innumerable small holes in the rocks are an ideal habitat for fish that tend to conceal themselves, like the moray, which, in most cases, only shows its head. Watch globefish, breams, groupers, stingrays and cuttlefish swimming about in their natural habitat. The whales which occasionally pass by off the coast of Tenerife will only be spotted if you're very lucky.

As many nocturnal shellfish use those small rock holes as their hideaways, there is also much to be discoverd at night. Afficianados of wreck-diving might profit from a visit to the wreck of a sunken ship off Los Cristianos, as well as that of a DC3 airplane which crashed into the sea near Puerto de la Cruz.

There are diving schools on Tenerife in all the major holiday resorts, such as Los Cristianos, Puerto de Las Américas, Los Gigantes and Puerto de la Cruz. Usually the diving areas are located in the immediate vicinity of the coast, with the two

notable exceptions of the small villages of Radazul and Santa María del Mar. They are located a few kilometers to the south of the capital Santa Cruz, and can be reached via the freeway from the diving schools.

The prices for diving are pretty much in the medium price range: a guided dive with complete rental equipment costs around US $30. If you bring your own equipment along, you'll usually get a discount of a couple of dollars. For transport by boat and nighttime diving courses, they generally charge you an extra 20 percent or so. You are qualified to participate in courses if you have a diving certificate and a medical certificate showing a clean bill of health. Allow four to five days for courses which accord with the international standards of CMAS and PADI; the costs amount to around US $225 including equipment.

Very much in demand are also so-called "sample courses," which are offered by diving schools in the hotel swimming pools.

Deep-Sea Fishing

The diversity of marine fauna is what deep-sea anglers find so attractive about the waters around Tenerife. Only two nautical miles off the coast, marlin, tuna, swordfish, and various shark species can be found. Be aware: Vacationers hoping to reel in the fish of their dreams on board a captained ship will be disappointed, for the captain always claims the prize catch for himself. Only small fish may be taken from the boat.

Most boats put to sea from the harbor in Los Gigantes. In order to get an idea of the usual catches, it is worthwhile watching the boats enter the harbor from about 2 o'clock in the afternoon onwards. There is no guarantee, however, that the same result will be achieved on the following day. It is recommended that you compare the rates of a number of companies before booking your fishing trip. Make sure that no more than three fishermen are going to be on one boat, otherwise you are almost guaranteed to get in each other's way.

CANARIAN CUISINE
Substantial and Delicious

The Canary Islands have been one of the most popular vacation destinations with Europeans for decades now, so it's no surprise to encounter dishes from all the tourists' countries of origin when you go out to eat in the large resorts here. With all the Irish pubs and Bierkellers everywhere, it's hard to find anything authentically Canarian.

If you really want to get to know Canarian cuisine, you'll need to head inland. Restaurants can be divided into three categories: simple, small ones with good home cooking; large excursion places with meat and seafood specialties, where local families take all their relations at weekends; and rather expensive gourmet establishments where refined Canarian cuisine is served to those able to afford it.

Above: Mojo, a dip that comes in a number of variations, gofio and watercress soup are all important components of Canarian cooking. Right: Dried fish is often offered for sale right in the harbor.

Canarian cuisine originated as the rural cooking of the Spanish and Portuguese immigrants, enriched by influences from Latin America. The wealthier households enjoyed produce grown on their own estates, or imported from overseas. Very filling meat dishes and sweet desserts were a regular feature of every main meal, and still are today. In the coastal towns seafood, simply but deliciously prepared in a variety of ways, was the main dish. Day laborers and their wives often had to rely on *gofio* and potatoes as basic foodstuffs. *Gofio*, roast flour made of wheat, maize or chickpeas, is one of the few foods that still dates back to the times of the Guanches.

Each household had (and still has) its own recipe for the typical sauce known as *mojo*, of which there are four basic types: a spicy mojo, with small red chili peppers marinated in olive oil and wine vinegar (*mojo picón* or *mojo rojo*); a green mojo with herbs (*mojo verde*); a garlic-dip mojo (*mojo de ajo*); and finally a saffron mojo with oregano and garlic (*mojo de azafrán*).

Tapas, those delicious Spanish appetizers, are available in almost all the restaurants and bars on the islands. They can range from cheese with olives to ham, vegetables, fish and meat, all served in delicious sauces.

Thick Soups and Hearty Stews

A soup is often served before the main course. There are various kinds of fish soup, and also vegetable soups known as *potajes*, which are usually very thick because of their high potato content. Pumpkins, cabbages and beans are also popular ingredients. One popular soup of the day is *sopa de berros*, made from watercress. If you order a *sopa de garbanzos* (chickpea soup) you'd better be hungry, because it's often as filling as an entire meal.

Stews play a great role in Canary Island cookery. A *puchero canario* contains up to seven different kinds of meat, all cooked with tomatoes, carrots, onions and chickpeas. Together with that there's a broth composed of beans, white cabbage, yellow squash, sweet corn, sweet potatoes and taro root. To spice things up a bit the locals use crushed garlic cloves, pepper, cloves, oil, and – if you want a really filling meal – some salted meat and *chorizo,* a smoked red sausage. Sliced pears or other fruit may also be added.

First you eat meat and vegetables; then you take some *gofio* flour out of a bowl and roll it into balls before dipping it into whatever sauce you have left on your plate – it's a delicious and very filling side dish. Whatever sauce is left behind after the *gofio* is eaten with a spoon.

Other stews include *sancocho*, a simple vegetable stew which is usually livened up with meat or fish (usually dried fish), and *olla potrida*, which usually consists of beef, sausage and vegetables.

Marinated Rabbit

It's virtually the Canarian national dish: marinated rabbit with boiled potatoes (*conejo en salmorejo con papas arrugadas*). The rabbit is left to marinate in a mixture of garlic, parsley, oregano, thyme, paprika, salt, pepper, oil and vinegar for at least one night. Then it gets basted in a ceramic pot until the flesh almost falls from the bone, while being sprinkled at intervals with wine. Small, whole potatoes are served as a side dish, boiled in their skins in a pot of seawater, so they crinkle up and get a shiny white crust of sea salt.

Fresh Seafood

Delicious fresh fish is served in the fishing villages of all the Canary Islands, and in the best restaurants you can choose it for yourself. The range on offer usually includes hake (*merluza*), angler fish (*sama*), sole (*lenguado*), sea bass (*mero*) and a kind of brace (*vieja*). On top of that

they have tuna fish steaks (*atún*), swordfish (*pez espada*) and also shark (*tiburón*). Try the brace baked in salt, too (*dorada a la sal*).

If you're not that hungry, and don't mind such things, there's octopus (*pulpo*) and squid (*calamares*), marinated as *tapas*. From depths of up to 700 meters they catch shrimps (*cangrejos*), prawns (*gambas*) and lobster, including the elongated *langostas canarias*. If you're unfamiliar with dried cod (*bacalao*), only eat it if it's recommended.

Desserts

After the meal, before coffee and/or *coñac*, Canarios indulge in a sweet and usually high-calorie dessert (*postre*). The flambéed bananas are filling, as are *turrón de gofio*, an almond dessert made of honey, flour and figs, *bienmesabe*, a sweet dish made of eggs and almonds, and *frangollo*, which is made of maize and milk. Alternatively you can have a piece of fresh fruit.

Above: Tuna fish, fresh from the boat. Right: Checking the wine's color as a prelude to tasting it.

Cheese

Smoked and unsmoked sheep and goat cheese is produced on all the islands; it usually tastes strong and slightly salty. The simple goat's cheese *queso blanco* is served almost everywhere. A local specialty is the mild cheese known as "flower cheese" (*queso de flor*) from Gran Canaria, produced in Guía from fresh sheep and cow's milk. This flower cheese – which gets its name from the bluish-purple artichoke flowers used in its production – comes in three stages of ripeness: *tierno* (soft/young), *semiduro* (half ripe) and *viejo* (old), and is very delicious indeed. Incidentally, there's usually a very broad assortment of cheeses on sale at any of the markets, and you can also ask the farmers themselves what kind they produce.

Drink

The mineral water (*agua mineral*) on the islands is good, and can be ordered either *con gas* or *sin gas* (carbonated or non-carbonated). The fruit juices (*zumos de fruta*) are usually freshly squeezed, and the milkshakes (*batidos*) are often mixed with ice cream or fruit. A particularly creamy and interesting one is the light-green *batido de aguacate*, which is made from avocados.

For warmer temperatures, assuming it's drunk in moderation, the local beer (*cerveza*) is ideal; it comes in two brands, "Dorada" and "Tropical." At mealtimes, wines from Lanzarote and Tenerife are recommended; good-quality Spanish mainland wines are also available. There's a choice between *vino tinto* (red), *rosado* (rosé) and *blanco* (white). The quality of a Rioja is often better than that of a local Canarian wine, but sometimes there are some delicious surprises. The whites from Lanzarote have a very special flavor, deriving from the volcanic soil. To go with coffee afterwards, instead of a dessert wine you can also try *ron miel*, a honey rum, or a banana liqueur (*crema de banana*). Restaurants attached to wine estates often serve *Aguardiente de Parra*, a clear spirit distilled on the premises.

If you feel like coffee after the meal, you can have a *café solo*, an ordinary small black espresso, or a *café doble* which is the same thing only twice as big. If there's a little milk inside, it becomes a *café cortado*, which is far more popular with the locals than regular coffee with milk (*café con leche*). German-style filter coffee is also available in some places as *café alemán*.

In the tourist centers, exotic cocktails are ubiquitous. All the known types, from Planter's Punches to Singapore Slings – get brought to tables with sparklers attached to them. One simpler and yet equally good cocktail is a *Mojito Cubano*, a mixture of Havana rum and fresh mint which was brought back here from Cuba by returning emigrants.

ARTS AND CRAFTS ON THE CANARY ISLANDS

The steady increase in visitors to the Canary Islands has also resulted in an expanding market for souvenirs, especially typical arts and crafts products made on the islands. Professions that were threatened with extinction during the industrial age have been given a new lease of life by tourism, and are often state-subsidized into the bargain.

Roseta

Vilaflor or Tenerife lace, very time-consuming to make and very beautiful, was an export article as long ago as the 19th century. *Roseta* is the name given to it because the basic form is a rosette, although there are numerous variations, including stylized fish, butterflies or flowers. Several of the rosettes can be joined together to make a tablecloth, and the women often work for years on end to create valuable cloaks and mantillas. Despite competition from China, which has been mass-producing the same thing, Rosetas on Tenerife are still made by hand: in Vilaflor, La Escalona, Arona, Valle de San Lorenzo, San Miguel and Granadilla. The preferred color for the lacework is white or a natural color, though black is always the color chosen for a mantilla. On Lanzarote (in San Bartolomé, Teguise and Tinajo) the women usually produce their rosetas in blue, green and yellow.

Calados

Traditional hem-stitch embroidery (*Calados*) involves removing a number of strands from a cloth and then turning the fronds into attractive and subtle patterns which are usually geometrical. Calados centers on Tenerife are all located along the north coast, from Victoria de Acentejo as far as Buenavista. In Orotava young women are trained in the art at the Casas de los Balcones, so the tradition doesn't die out. A common pattern in the south of Tenerife, in the villages of Fasnia, Granadilla, Chimiche and El Escobonal, is a spidery one known as *arañón.* The bastions of calados on Gran Canaria are Gáldar and Moya in the north, and Ingenio, Agüímes and San Bartolomé de Tirajana in the south. Traditional centers on Fuerteventura, alongside the capital, are Lajares, La Oliva, Tindaya, La Mantilla and Tetir in the north, and Betancuria, Triquivijate, Antigua, Los Llanos and Casillas del Ángel in the center.

Right: In the Casa de los Balcones in Orotava, a basket-maker shows his skill.

Silk

El Paso on La Palma was once a silk production center with its own silkworm farm and numerous mulberry trees. All that remains today is a small factory that makes ties, scarves and handkerchiefs, and it is run by Doña Bertila Pérez González. All the silkworms come from Japan, and live in shoeboxes full of mulberry leaves. Señora Bertila, who has received several awards for her services to the silk industry, can explain each phase of the process to you. She colors her material with natural dyes.

Basketry and Weaving

Wherever the Canary Islands have preserved their original, rural character, basket weaving still plays a role; straw, reeds and palm leaves are all used as materials. The latter are used to make artistic decorations frequently encountered at church festivals, e.g., Palm Sunday. The finely-woven straw hats from Yaiza and Tinajo on Lanzarote are also an exquisite rarity, and are correspondingly difficult (and expensive) to get hold of. They make a perfect souvenir, however.

Pottery

The Guanches modeled their ceramic products without the use of a wheel, and this technique is still used in many places on the Canary Islands. There may not be any direct connection with the Guanches in this regard at all, in fact, but instead with immigrants who came here from Galicia, where pots were also made using this technique. In Victoria de Acentejo on Tenerife, some families still make ceramic vessels in the traditional manner; pottery is also produced in the museum of Arguayo, and in Santa Cruz de Tenerife there's an employment program called "Potting without a Wheel" (Centro Ocupacional San José Obrero, Calle Marisol Marín 5).

The pottery centers on Gran Canaria can be found at La Atalaya and Hoya de Pineda. Here, as well as in Santa Lucía de Tirajana, clay copies of ancient Guanche figures are also manufactured. The equivalent location on the island of La Palma is at Hoyo de Mazo, where potters can also be seen working away. On La Gomera, the most important ceramic production center is Chipude.

Cigars and Timples

Some craft centers, such as the Patio Limonero in Garachico on Tenerife, allow visitors to watch cigars being made by hand. There's also a modest homemade cigar business run by several old men in El Paso. Canarian cigars taste good, and if you're a smoker, or know any, they make excellent souvenirs.

A typically Canarian folk instrument is the *timple*, a kind of small guitar with a rounded soundboard, resembling a mandolin. The most famous timple factories in the Canary Islands can be found in Teguise (Lanzarote). Musical instruments such as guitars, chácaras and also tambourines are manufactured in La Orotava, Playa de San Juan (Tenerife), Taibique, Sabinosa, Guarazoca (El Hierro), Hermigua (La Gomera) and Telde (Gran Canaria).

FLORA AND FAUNA

The flora of the Canary Islands is utterly fascinating. It's not only the sheer variety of plants here that is so astonishing, but their size as well. The tiny poinsettia familiar from flowerpots in Europe grows to the size of a small tree here on the islands. There are around 3,000 different plant species on the Canaries. Many were introduced as useful plants or as ornamentals, while some traveled here as "stowaways" on board ships and went to seed. What makes the flora of the Canaries so exotic is not only the imported tropical plants but also the very high proportion of endemic varieties. Around 585 different plants are native to the islands, whereby around 370 species are endemic – i.e., they occur on just one island, and sometimes even in just one barranco.

Above: Aeonium holochrysum, an endemic, thick-leaved plant. Right: North African ground squirrel on Fuerteventura. Following pages: Sunset at the end of a great day's cycling.

The highest proportion of wild plants can be found on Tenerife and Gran Canaria, with 1,300 and 1,260 different species respectively; the lowest is Hierro, with 530 species. Tenerife occupies a special place among the islands in that its climatic zones enable a very large number of different plants to grow. It has 135 endemic species which have now been transferred to the neighboring islands. In this way, Tenerife has 21 of the same species as Gran Canaria, 65 kilometers away. Some of these endemic plants, including the legendary dragon tree, the Canarian laurel and several Canary ferns originate from the Tertiary Period, and can only be found in fossilized form in more northerly regions.

Dragon Trees and Euphorbias

The botanical symbol of the islands is the dragon tree (Spanish: *drago*), which was worshiped as a sacred tree back in the Guanche era. It isn't a tree at all actually, but a member of the lily family, and since it has no rings, guessing its age is not easy. When the bark is scratched it emits a colorless sap which goes dark red on exposure to the air. This liquid was used medicinally by the Guanches, and they also embalmed the bodies of their dead with it.

If you hike through the dry zones you'll encounter the endemic Candelabra euphorbia (Spanish: *cardón*), which, like all euphorbias, excretes a milky acidic juice. This also applies to its rather similar relative the King Juba euphorbia (*tabaiba*), recognizable by its reddish fruit capsules above a wreath of pointed leaves. It is believed that the Guanches used juice from this plant to anesthetize fish before catching them.

The Canary palm, which resembles a date palm, is extremely elegant. Its fruit is only eaten by birds and rats, and streetcleaners use its leaves as brooms. The Canary pine is important for the islands' water supply. It has needles up to 30 cen-

timeters in length which "comb" the fog up in the mountains, thereby providing the soil with moisture. It has also proven extremely resistant to forest fires.

The most unusual flower on the islands is the red Teide echium, which grows in the Cañadas at the foot of Mount Teide and blooms from May to early July. It grows as high as a man, and one plant can produce up to 84,000 red blossoms. Also known as "The Pride of Tenerife," it has now been successfully planted on Gran Canaria.

Few other plants manage to survive in the desert-like, arid landscape above the tree level, but one which does is *retama*, the pink-and-white Teide broom (*Spartocytisus nubigens*).

The author Miguel de Unamuno regarded the thorny lettuce (Spanish: *ahulaga*), though not endemic, as best embodying his vision of Fuerteventura as a dried-out, skeleton-like island. Adapted to suit a desert-like climate, this plant has reduced its leaves to the bare minimum: they have become thorns.

Lizards and Canaries

The Canary Islands only have a modest amount of wildlife. Domestic pets excepted, there are no large mammals apart from moufflons, a species of shaggy sheep imported several years ago. Their population has swelled since then, and because they threaten the flora on Mount Teide they are being hunted to keep their numbers down. Rabbits live wild, but usually land up on menus. More unusual fauna includes certain (harmless) reptiles, and also the giant lizard. The gecko (Spanish: *perenquén*) is a common sight in houses, and eats insects. There are several Canary lizards, one species of which lives on Hierro and grows to a length of 60 centimeters. Other native animals include the Canary skink.

The most famous bird, of course, is the canary. The wild ones don't sing at all, by the way; only when they're caged and taught to do so. Their plumage is also a subdued grayish-green, rather than dazzling yellow.

METRIC CONVERSION

Metric Unit	US Equivalent
Meter (m)	39.37 in.
Kilometer (km)	0.6241 mi.
Square Meter (sq m)	10.76 sq. ft.
Hectare (ha)	2.471 acres
Square Kilometer (sq km)	0.386 sq. mi.
Kilogram (kg)	2.2 lbs.
Liter (l)	1.05 qt.

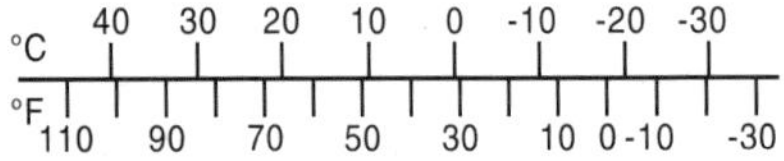

TRAVEL PREPARATIONS

Tourist Information

In the UK: Spanish Tourist Office, 57-58 St. James's Street, London SW1A 1LD, tel. (0171) 499-0901. For brochures, tel. (0891) 669920.

In the US: Tourist Office of Spain, 665 Fifth Avenue, New York, NY 10022, tel. (212) 759-8822; 8383 Wiltshire Boulevard, Suite 960, Beverly Hills, CA 90211, tel. (213) 658-7188; Water Tower Place, Suite 915 East, 845 North Michigan Avenue, Chicago, IL 60611, tel. (312) 642-1992, 944-0216, fax. (312) 642-9817; 1221 Brickell Avenue, Miami, FL 33131, tel. (305) 358-1992, fax. (305) 358-8223.

In Canada: 102 Bloor Street West, 14th Floor, Toronto, Ontario M5S 1M8, tel. (416) 961-3131, 961-4079, fax. (416) 961-1992.

In Australia: 203 Castlereagh Street, Level 2, Suite 21a, PO Box 675, 2000 Sydney, NSW, tel. (02) 264-7966.

Internet Addresses

The following Internet addresses can be very useful sources of additional information about to the Canary Islands:
Canary Islands: www.members.aol.com/canconsult/links.htm.
Tenerife: www.cabtfe.es/inicio/index2.asp.

Spanish Embassies

UK: Spanish Embassy, 20 Peel Street, London W8 7PD, tel. (0171) 727-2462, 243-8535, fax. (0171) 229-4965.

US: Consulate General of Spain in New York, 150 East 58th Street, New York, NY 10155, tel. (212) 355-4080, fax. (212) 644-3751.

Canada: 74 Stanley Avenue, Ottawa, Ontario, Canada K1M 1P4, tel. (613) 747-2252, fax. (613) 744-1224.

Entry Regulations

If planning to stay for up to three months, visitors need to have a valid passport. Anyone planning to stay longer than that needs to get a visa from the Spanish embassy or consulate in his or her native country.

Visa extensions while on the Canaries have to be applied for at the *Gobierno Civil* in Santa Cruz de Tenerife or Las Palmas de Gran Canaria. An application certification from the consulate of one's own country is needed for this, along with an application certificate for the municipality in which one intends to reside. In addition, one must show proof of having health insurance. In certain cases an adequate income has to be proven by bank guarantee.

Anyone arriving by ferry in their own car needs the green international insurance card, as well as the usual papers and driver's license.

For pets, such as cats and dogs, an official veterinary certificate is required to be shown which may not be older than two weeks and must confirm in both English and Spanish that the animal has been vaccinated against rabies within the past year, and at least one month before entry.

Health

The same guidelines apply for the Canary Islands as for Europe. Vaccinations against tetanus and polio might be considered. There are good pharmacies almost everywhere on the islands.

Many common medications are available from the pharmacies on the island, even though they may have different names here. If you bring along the paper normally enclosed with medications, or a at least a description of the medication from your physician, the Spanish pharmacist can generally work out what you need from that and provide you with the Spanish equivalent.

Under EU regulations, an E111 form should provide treatment for residents of Great Britain while on Tenerife. This can often lead to delays and red tape, however, so it's best to have your own private insurance if possible. American visitors should also check that their health insurance gives them adequate coverage, and take out an additional travel insurance policy if necessary.

The standard of health care in the hospitals here is first class, and many towns also have a facility that can provide first aid or emergency treatment. Most doctors speak good English.

Ambulances will take you to the nearest hospital that is available, which will treat your complaint, but many are private and will only treat you if you have private medical insurance – so it's very important to have the relevant documents.

Pharmacies can be recognized by the green or red Maltese crosses on the sign outside, and in the cities and larger towns there is always at least one emergency pharmacy open all night long (see also "Medical Treatment / Pharmacies," on page 89).

Clothing

For a pure beach holiday you'll be fine with just light summer clothing in both summer and winter; warmer clothing is only needed in the evenings, or if a wind blows up. Despite the mild temperatures on Tenerife, you should not underestimate the power of the sun – good sun protection is essential, especially if the weather is windy.

Even though casual clothing is usually okay, the better hotels on the islands consider etiquette important at mealtimes, and especially in the evenings, when more formal clothing is required; the same applies to expensive restaurants and cultural events.

Those who have chosen accommodation at higher altitudes (from 500 meters to over 1,500 meters), or are planning on hikes in the mountains, must expect repeated rain showers and cooler temperatures (up to 10°C cooler than on the coast). Bring along rain protection, a light sweater or jacket, and sturdy shoes for unsurfaced paths.

When to Go

Tenerife is a popular travel destination all year round. The peak season is during European vacation times, in the autumn, at Christmas, carnival time and Easter, and flights and accommodation have to be booked well in advance, often up to six months before your trip. In winter a lot of old-age pensioners come here to stay warm, while in the summer you're more likely to meet young and middle-aged people.

Currency Exchange / Regulations

Until it gives way to the Euro, the Spanish peseta (abbreviated "Pta") is the country's unit of currency. There are 20,000, 10,000, 5,000, 2,000 and 1,000 Pta banknotes; 500, 200, 100, 50, 25, 10, 5, 2 and 1 Pta coins. The 5-Pta coin is known familiarly as a *duro*.

The current exchange rate is:

US $1	174 Ptas
UK £1	278 Ptas
AUS $1	106 Ptas

Incidentally, a little sound financial advice: Only exchange a small amount of pesetas at home, enough to keep you until you can get to a bank, because the exchange rate on the island is usually a lot better. Any amount of foreign currency can be brought with you to Tenerife. If you want to take out large sums of money, it's best to declare it – because the maximum permissible amount per person without declaration is up to one million pesetas and foreign currency with an equivalent value of 500,000 Ptas.

There are automatic cash dispensers at all the holiday resorts and large towns (on Hierro in Valverde and Frontera). Traveler's checks, cash and Eurochecks can be exchanged at any bank. Credit cards are accepted nearly everywhere – apart from Hierro, where they are the exception to the rule (see also "Banks," page 88).

ARRIVAL

By Plane

A lot of European charter flights go directly to the Canary Islands. Tenerife is also served by larger airlines, such as British Airways, Air France, Iberia, Lufthansa, Swissair, etc.

In general, package tours are cheaper than holidays tailored to one's own preferences – and so comparing prices and offers by various travel agents is always a good idea. Most charter flights allow 20 kilograms of luggage, though if you're planning to stay longer you can apply to have the amount increased.

Special luggage (such as sports equipment) has to be reported in good time; a bicycle or surfboard usually costs around US $50-75 extra. If you want to take your pets along too (in special containers), that has to be officially applied for as well. The price of the journey is based on the weight of the animal.

Passport checks are quite rare within the EU, which saves a lot of time and hassle, and luggage is only examined in special cases (suspected weapons or drugs, etc.). The procedure is a lot stricter for intercontinental flights.

In the arrivals hall you will find rental car companies, automatic cash dispensers, tourist information, a post office and a currency exchange outlet.

Just after arrival at the airport is a good time to exchange your currency for pesetas – you might be surprised at how favorable the rates are.

By Ship

From Cádiz (on mainland Spain) a ferry of the *Companía Trasmediterránea* arrives every Saturday, with stops in Santa Cruz de Tenerife (the trip takes around 40 hours).

In the summer you have to book months in advance, mainly because of the relative lack of transportation capacity for automobiles.

Timetables, prices and applications can be obtained from **Companía Transmediterránea**, Plaza Manuel Gómez Moreno, E-28020 Madrid, tel. 91423-8500 or 91423-8832. Branch office: Avda. Ramón de Carranza 26/7, E-11006 Cádiz, tel. 95628-7850.

ISLAND-HOPPING

By Plane

Flights run by Iberia and its subsidiaries, or by other private firms, travel between the islands several times a day, and no flight takes longer than one hour. These flights can be booked at travel agencies at home, at the agencies in the Canary Islands themselves, from Iberia (also for its subsidiaries) or directly at the airports.

A large amount of domestic air traffic operates from the Los Rodeos airport on Tenerife, near La Laguna in the north, which is slightly bothersome if you want a connecting international flight from Aeropuerto Reina Sofía in the south.

By Ship

The cheapest way of getting from Point A to Point B is to "island-hop" by ferry. All the islands are connected by car ferry, though not always directly. Some routes, such as those between Tenerife and Gran Canaria, and between Tenerife and

Gomera, are served by jetfoils, but these are senstive to choppy seas and don't always run.

Competing for ferry traffic are the state-run *Companía Trasmediterránea* (Las Palmas de Gran Canaria, tel. 928-260070; see p. 86), its subsidiary *Naviera Armas* (Las Palmas de Gran Canaria, tel. 928-474080) and the private shipping company *Líneas Fred Olsen* (Santa Cruz de Tenerife, tel. 922-628200). The price differences between all three are minimal. Tickets can be booked via travel agencies or at the companies' respective harbor offices. Tickets are usualy still available just before departures apart from on public holidays, so booking ahead isn't always a must.

TRAFFIC CONNECTIONS ON TENERIFE

By Bus

All the islands have efficient public bus service networks. On Tenerife there is one large bus company, which has squeezed out private competition and which services the entire island. Larger towns are served several times a day, but small villages aren't always part of the network (see the *INFO* section on pages 53-59).

Timetables are available at larger bus terminals, near tourist offices, at the airports or in the vacation resorts. Group tickets and multiple-journey tickets can often be a lot cheaper than the usual rate.

By Taxi

Taxicabs are relatively inexpensive on Tenerife, but it's always best to settle on a price with the driver before you start to move. For overland trips it's a good idea to ask for a look at the list of fixed tariffs. As a rule, one kilometer costs 100 pesetas, though short trips are a bit more expensive. There's also an official surcharge for trips on Sundays and public holidays.

By Rental Car

Rental cars in the economy car category cost a weekly rate of between 2,200 and 2,500 pesetas a day, plus insurance of around 1,200 pesetas a day. If you're staying longer you can generally negotiate a better rate. The international car rental companies will organize your car for you before you leave on vacation, but it's also possible to take advantage of local competitiveness and negotiate a deal with the smaller companies on the islands themselves. If you do find a cheap offer, make sure the vehicle is roadworthy, and also check the size of the rental fleet – just so you don't have to waste two valuable days of your vacation waiting around for a substitute vehicle that never appears.

A national driver's license is sufficient for renting a car. There is often a clause in the contract that says the driver has to be at least 21 years old. If you want others to drive as well as you, their names have to be entered in the contract and their respective licenses shown, too.

Hitchhiking

On the island the locals hitchhike quite a lot, but that's usually because they know the drivers passing them. Tourists have a much harder time of thumbing a ride.

Traffic Regulations

Basically the traffic regulations are the same as the rest of Europe. Cars drive on the right, and seat-belts have to be fastened, even in town traffic. The alcohol limit is 0.8 – and police checks are particularly frequent late at night whenever there's a fiesta on. At traffic circles, unless otherwise indicated, the vehicle arriving from the right has priority.

If you suddenly have to slow down or stop because of an obstacle in the road, you can warn the driver behind by switching on your left indicator or sticking your left hand out of the window. On winding mountain roads it's always best to sound the horn before a bend.

In the Canary Islands the speed limit in built-up areas is 60 kph, on country roads 90 kph, on major roads 100 kph and on highways 120 kph. On weekends some people tend to travel amazingly quickly, and enjoy overtaking on bends, but most of the local drivers are generally very courteous and obliging.

PRACTICAL TIPS FROM A TO Z

Accommodation

Most accommodation is geared towards package tours; individual travelers who haven't booked in advance won't find it easy to find suitable and inexpensive accommodation in the tourist centers during peak season. Tourist information offices in the islands provide lists with prices and descriptions.

The Spanish authorities have divided hotels, boarding houses and apartments into categories, but these only apply to furnishings. So the number of stars or key symbols an establishment may have says nothing about the actual quality of the service and the atmosphere there.

The official categories for hotels range from luxury (5-star) to simple (1-star); for apartments from high-class (3-star) to simple (1-star) and for boarding houses from pleasant family-run establishments (2-star) to very simple places (1-star) with shared bathrooms and lavatories. The categories in the *INFO* section on pages 50-53 have attempted to take atmosphere and service into account as well. The prices are based on the following scale: $ Simple: Double rooms up to 5,000 pesetas. $$ Medium: Double rooms from 5,000 to 10,000 pesetas. $$$ Luxury: Double rooms over 10,000 pesetas.

If you're interested in vacationing in a **Finca** (a country farmhouse, often recently renovated), your local travel agency at home or one of the offices on the islands can provide you with further details. The EU project *Turismo Rural*, whereby old buildings are being renovated and turned into holiday homes, offers good places.

Camping is not very widespread on Tenerife. Some beaches have become unofficial campsites, but this is just a tolerated exception to the rule. Communal or private campsites outside the nature reserves are rare, and not usually very peaceful. Camping without a permit is naturally forbidden inside the nature reserves, and even at the official locations you still have to get a permit in advance from the environmental or national park authorities (tourist offices provide more information on this). It's worth making the extra effort to get the permit, however, because of the beauty of the sites. Never camp in narrow ravines (*barrancos*) however – they're prone to falling rocks and boulders!

Banks

Banks are open Monday through Friday from 9 a.m. to 2 p.m., Saturdays to 1 p.m., and slightly longer in summer and during carnival season. If you're exchanging cash or traveler's checks (maximum 25,000 pesetas per check), remember that rates and commissions vary from bank to bank. Exchange outlets and hotels (unfavorable rates!) will change money and checks outside banking hours. Credit cards are accepted almost everywhere, automatic cash dispensers are also a common sight (see "Currency Exchange," pp. 85-86). If you lose checks or credit cards, block them instantly.

Crime

The Canary Islands are generally regarded as relatively safe. Violent crime is rare, but petty crime does exist, especially on the large islands with all the tourism, urban poverty and drug problems. If you leave your car parked in a remote location, make sure you take all valuables out – and also leave the glove compartment open so that it's clear the car has nothing inside. Deposit your valuables in the hotel safe, especially in vacation villages. Also beware of free trips to buy cheap goods. If you agree to one of these, make sure you can assess the quality of what you're offered and check whether it might not be cheaper at home. The best-case scenario here is usually the loss of one day's vacation. If you get taken to a time-sharing location, don't sign anything resembling a contract. Proper firms allow people plenty of time to consider the whole thing, and provide consultations with experts and legal advisers.

On some very busy promenades you may get tricked out of your cash by professional tricksters (e.g., shell games) working together with seemingly uninvolved bystanders.

Customs Regulations

As long as the Canary Islands are not fully integrated into the EU, the customs regulations for entrance into the EU are the same for those of a non-EU state: the duty-free allowances are 200 cigarettes (or 100 cigarillos or 50 cigars or 250 grams of tobacco), one liter of spirits, and two liters of wine.

Once the islands have been fully integrated into the EU, and assuming no special regulations apply, the duty-free limit for import into an EU country will be 800 cigarettes (or 400 cigarillos or 200 cigars) and 90 liters of wine (or 10 liters of spirits or 20 liters of liqueur).

Disabled Assistance

The *Fundación OID* (*Organización Impulsora de Discapacitados*) in Santa Cruz de Tenerife provides help and information for the disabled, tel. 922-202886. *Le Ro* looks after the disabled and rents out electric wheelchairs. Los Cristianos, Edificio Mar y Sol, tel. 922-750289.

Electricity

The tourist centers have the two round pin sockets familiar from France and Germany, so bring an adapter. Current is 220 volts. Some places still have 110 to 125 volts AC with sockets that need an extra adapter, too.

Emergencies

The emergency number to call on Tenerife is 092. For first aid or a medic, call 061. The number for the fire department is 080.

Gratuities

In bars and restaurants service is generally included in the bill, but good service is rewarded with a gratuity of around 10 percent of the price. In hotels, chambermaids and porters are given a suitable amount on arrival and departure, especially if they clearly go out of their way to assist. Cab drivers expect around 10 percent of the fare. Outside the tourist centers, people are more ready to help without shooting calculating glances at your wallet.

Medical Treatment / Pharmacies

Medical treatment on the island is good almost everywhere. The hospitals are of European standards. Hotel receptions, tour operators or the consulate will give you the location of the nearest emergency station or medical practice. Many towns and even some small villages have first aid stations operated by the Red Cross (*Cruz Roja*).

Pharmacies (*farmacias*; normally with a green or red Maltese cross on the sign), are open Monday through Friday from 9 a.m. to 1 p.m. and 4 to 8 p.m., and Sat from 9 a.m. to 1 p.m. Pharmacies in every large town have night and emergency opening hours (*Farmacia de Guardia*). The signs outside them tell you which one is currently open.

Thanks to good hygiene conditions, visitors hardly ever get sick. The most common ailments are caused by the change in climate and in diet. Give your body some time to adapt – avoid overdoing things on day one, eat food that's easily digestible, and drink a lot of liquids, but not too much alcohol (if at all). Avoid long periods of sunbathing without proper protection. The tap water is perfectly okay, and you can brush your teeth with it without worry (see also "Health," pp. 84-85).

Opening Times

There are no firmly fixed opening times for businesses. Most stores are open Monday through Friday from 9 a.m. to 1 p.m. and 4:30 to 7:30 p.m., and Saturdays from 9 a.m. to 2 p.m. In the vacation resorts these times are more flexible depending on the season and the amount of business, and some stores are even open on Sundays.

Photography

A large selection of film material is available in the tourist centers, but it's rather more expensive than in other parts of Europe or the U.S. Check the "sell-by" date. Film is also developed overnight in the tourist centers, and the prices are moderate.

Post Offices (Correo)

Generally speaking, all the windows are open in post offices from Monday through Saturday (9 a.m. to 1 p.m., also the one for general delivery). In the big towns the main post offices are also open in the afternoons, and some don't even break for lunch.

Stamps for normal letters and postcards cost 65 pesetas for EU countries, 75 pesetas for non-EU European countries, and 95 pesetas for overseas destinations. Stamps can also be purchased at tobacconists, souvenir stores and hotels.

Public Holidays

The following are official public holidays in the Canary Islands:

January 1: New Year's Day (*Año Nuevo*).
January 6: Epiphany (*Los Reyes*).
March 19: St. Joseph's Day (*San José*).
May 1: Labor Day (*Día del Trabajo*).
May 30: Canaries Day (*Día de Canarias*).
July 25: St. Jacob's Day (*Santiago*).
August 15: Assumption Day (*Asunción*).
October 12: Day of the Spanish-Speaking World (*Día de la Hispanidad*).
November 1: All Saints' Day (*Todos los Santos*).
December 6: Constitution Day (*Día de la Constitución*).
December 8: Immaculate Conception (*Immaculada Concepción*).
December 25: Christmas (*Navidad*).
Moveable Feasts: Maundy Thursday, Good Friday, Easter, Whitsun, Ascension Day and Corpus Christi. Easter Monday, Whit Monday and Boxing Day are not public holidays in Spain.

The tourist offices on the individual islands provide more detailed information on religious festivals, pilgrimages and carnivals.

Swimming / Nude Sunbathing

Swimming in lonely bays without surveillance can be very dangerous because of the powerful undertow and often sharp rocks. The surf can be tricky, especially on the windward side of the island. On beaches where there is surveillance, signal flags tell you whether swimming is currently forbidden (red flag), only recommended for experienced swimmers (yellow flag) or allowed for everyone (green flag). Especially clean beaches fly blue EU flags.

You'll need to wear beach sandals in the black sand here, because it gets very hot – and footwear is also useful as protection against stones when you enter the water. Sun protection is essential.

In most tourist centers, topless bathing has become a regular feature on the beach and by the pool. Nude sunbathing is severely frowned upon, though, and is only tolerated on the beach near El Médano.

Telecommunications

You can dial abroad directly from phone booths bearing the words *internacional* or *interurbana*, either with coins or with phone cards. The latter, known as *tarjetas telefónicas*, are sold in 1,000 and 2,000 peseta versions from post offices, kiosks and souvenir stores. In the tourist centers you can also make phone calls from public phone offices (*teléfonos publicos*) without using coins. The number of units simply gets added up at the end of the call.

The code for dialing abroad from Spain is 07. After you hear a beep, dial the country code followed by the area code minus the initial zero, then the phone number itself.

No code is needed for calls within the island. The previous code, 922, has become a fixed part of the number now.

National directory assistance can be reached at 003, and international information at 025. From Europe to the Canaries you dial 0034 for Spain and then the number.

Time

The time on Tenerife is the same as that in the U.K., i.e., Greenwich Mean Time, or one hour behind Central European Time, and changes over at summertime as well – so there is no need for English visitors to adjust their watches.

PHRASEBOOK

The official language on the Canary Islands is Spanish. In tourist centers you'll find that most people understand English pretty well, but a basic knowledge of Spanish is useful if you travel inland.

All words ending with a vowel, an "s" or an "n" and without any accent, always have their penultimate syllable stressed. All other words are either stressed on the syllable with the accent or – if there isn't an accent – on the last syllable. For instance, *Los Cristianos* = los cristiAnos; *El Escobonal* = el escobonAl; *Andén Verde* = andEn vErde. Syllables with non-accented diphthongs count as one syllable, e.g., *Antigua* = antIgua; but: *Garafía* = garafIa.

General Expressions

Good morning . . . . *Buenos días*
Good afternoon . . . . . *Buenas tardes*
Good evening (early evening). . *Buenas tardes*
Good night . . . . *Buenas noches*
Hello! (between friends). . . . . *¡Hola!*
Goodbye . . . . *Hasta la vista*
Bye . . . . *Adiós*
See you later . . . . *Hasta luego*
See you tomorrow . . . . *Hasta mañana*
How are you?. . . . . *¿Qué tal?*
Thanks a lot . . . . . . *Muchas gracias*
Not at all . . . . *De nada*
Please . . . . *Por favor*
Go ahead . . . . *Sirvase Usted*
Excuse me . . . . *Perdón*
Yes . . . . *Sí*
No . . . . *No*
Do you speak English?. . *¿Habla Usted inglés?*
I don't understand Spanish . . . . . *No entiendo español*
Speak more slowly please . . . *Un poco mas despacio, por favor*
What's your name? . . *¿Cómo se llama Usted?*
My name is ... . *Me llamo ...*
I live in .... *Vivo en ...*
(Very) good . . . . *(Muy) bien*
Help! . . . . *¡Socorro!*
Turn left . . . . *A la izquierda*
Turn right . . . . *A la derecha*
Keep straight on . . . . *Siempre derecho*
How far is that? . *¿A qué distancia está?*
What time is it? . . . . . *¿Qué hora es?*
Up . . . . *Arriba*
Down . . . . *Abajo*
Here . . . . *Aquí*
There . . . . *Allí*
Who?. . . . . *¿Quién?*
Where? . . . . *¿Dónde?*
Where to? . . . . *¿Adonde?*

When? . . . . *¿Cuándo?*
How much?. . . . . *¿Cuánto?*
Where can I get ...? . . *¿Dónde hay ...?*
What does that cost? . . . *¿Cuánto vale esto? ¿Cuanto cuesta?*
The menu please! . . . . . . *¡La lista de platos! ¡El menú, por favor!*
The bill please! . *¡La cuenta, por favor!*
Do you have a room free? . . . . *¿Tiene Usted una habitación libre?*
Double Room. . . . . *Habitación doble*
Single Room. . . *Habitación individual*
Room with bath . *Habitación con baño*
For one night . . . . . . *Para una noche*
For one week . . . . . *Para una semana*
Can I see the room? . . . *¿Puedo ver la habitación?*
I want to rent a car. . . . . . . *Quisiera alquilar un coche*
I want to rent a boat . . . . . . *Quisiera alquilar una barca*
Yesterday. . . . . *Ayer*
Today . . . . *Hoy*
Tomorrow . . . . *Mañana*
Last night . . . . *Anoche*
Day after tomorrow . . *Pasado mañana*
Day before yesterday . . . . . *Anteayer*
Holiday . . . . *Día festivo*

Days of the Week

Monday. . . . . *Lunes*
Tuesday . . . . *Martes*
Wednesday . . . . *Miércoles*
Thursday . . . . *Jueves*
Friday . . . . *Viernes*
Saturday. . . . . *Sábado*
Sunday . . . . *Domingo*

Months

January . . . . *Enero*
February . . . . *Febrero*
March . . . . *Marzo*
April . . . . *Abril*
May . . . . *Mayo*
June . . . . *Junio*
July . . . . *Julio*
August . . . . *Agosto*
September . . . . *Setiembre*
October . . . . *Octubre*
November . . . . *Noviembre*
December . . . . *Diciembre*

In a Restaurant

Today's menu . . . . *Menú del día*
Dessert . . . . *Postre*
Bread . . . . *Pan*
Butter . . . . *Mantequilla*
Drink . . . . *Bebida*
Wine . . . . *Vino*
Beer . . . . *Cerveza*
Mineral water. . . . . . . *Agua mineral*
Carbonated/uncarbonated . *Con/sin gas*
Black coffee. . . . . *Café solo*
Coffee with a little milk. . *Café cortado*
Milk coffee . . . . *Café con leche*
Breakfast . . . . *Desayuno*
Lunch . . . . *Almuerzo*
Supper . . . . *Cena*
Sandwich . . . . *Bocadillo*
Omelette . . . . *Tortilla*
Potato omelette . . . . *Tortilla Española*
Soup . . . . *Sopa*
Meat . . . . *Carne*
Beef . . . . *Carne de Vaca*
Pork. . . . . *Cerdo*
Veal . . . . *Ternera*
Chicken . . . . *Pollo*
Lamb . . . . *Cordero*
Fried . . . . *Frito*
Grilled . . . . *A la plancha*
Baked. . . . . *Asado*
Salad . . . . *Ensalada*
Vegetables . . . . *Verdura*
Peas and beans . . . . *Legumbres*
Fish. . . . . *Pescado*
Sea pike . . . . *Merluza*
Trout. . . . . *Trucha*
Salmon . . . . *Salmón*
Tuna . . . . *Atún*
Swordfish . . . . *Pez espada*
Squid . . . . *Calamares*
Octopus . . . . *Pulpo*

Numbers

0 . . . . *cero*
1 . . . . *un(o), una*
2 . . . . *dos*
3 . . . . *tres*

4	*cuatro*
5	*cinco*
6	*seis*
7	*siete*
8	*ocho*
9	*nueve*
10	*diez*
11	*once*
12	*doce*
13	*trece*
14	*catorce*
15	*quince*
16	*dieciséis*
17	*diecisiete*
18	*dieciocho*
19	*diecinueve*
20	*veinte*
21	*veintiún(o/a)*
22	*veintidós*
30	*treinta*
31	*treinta y uno*
40	*cuarenta*
50	*cincuenta*
60	*sesenta*
70	*setenta*
80	*ochenta*
90	*noventa*
100	*cien(to)*
101	*ciento uno*
200	*doscientos/-as*
300	*trescientos/-as*
400	*cuatrocientos/-as*
500	*quinientos/-as*
600	*seiscientos/-as*
700	*setecientos/-as*
800	*ochocientos/-as*
900	*novecientos/-as*
1,000	*mil*
2,000	*dos mil*
3,000	*tres mil*
10,000	*diez mil*
100,000	*cien mil*
500,000	*quinientos mil*
1,000,000	*un millón (de)*

AUTHORS

Heiner Schwarz is an art historian who also studied Romance languages and literature. He has been regularly traveling to the Canary Islands for the past 20 years as a photographer and travel book author. Up to now he has written three books on Tenerife for various publishers. For this book he wrote the chapter "Tenerife – A Continent in Itself," as well as the features "Canarian Cuisine," "Arts and Crafts on the Canary Islands" and "Flora and Fauna."

Michael Reimer is a photographer and the author of a number of travel, hiking and cycling guides, as well as numerous articles published in trade journals. He wrote the "Historical Overview," as well as the feature "Cycling on Tenerife."

Wolfgang Taschner is a specialized freelance journalist as well as a travel guide author. He generally concentrates his writings on the field of active nature holidays. He has written numerous books on the Canary Islands, which are among his favorite travel destinations. For this book he contributed his expertise and experience in the features "The Sendero Turistico" and "Water Sports."

PHOTOGRAPHERS

Amberg, Gunda	19, 47
Amberg, Dr. Hellmuth	46
Bildagentur Dr. Wagner (Silvestris)	25
Brockhaus, Volkmar (Silvestris)	10/11
Eisenschink, Gerhard	62/63, 67, 69, 70, 82/83,
Fuchs, Don (Montanus)	3, 12/13, 24, 28, 38, 42, 49, 65, 66
Gruschwitz, Bernd	8, 14, 18, 26, 34, 37, 48
Heine, Heiner (Silvestris)	20, 21
Holzbachova, R., **Bénet**, P.	60/61
Lange, Harald (Silvestris)	cover
Nowak, Gerald	73
Pansegrau, Erhard	23, 35, 44, 45, 51
Schneider & Will (Silvestris)	27, 50
Stadler, Hubert	29, 31, 39, 43
Stankiewitz, Thomas	32, 33
Taschner, Wolfgang	9
Wolfsperger, Klaus (Montanus)	52.

Explore the World

NELLES MAPS

AVAILABLE TITELS

Afghanistan 1 : 1 500 000
Argentina *(Northern),* **Uruguay** 1 : 2 500 000
Argentina *(Southern),* **Uruguay** 1 : 2 500 000
Australia 1 : 4 000 000
Bangkok - *and Greater Bangkok* 1 : 75 000 / 1 : 15 000
Burma → *Myanmar*
Caribbean - **Bermuda, Bahamas, Greater Antilles** 1 : 2 500 000
Caribbean - **Lesser Antilles** 1 : 2 500 000
Central America 1 : 1 750 000
Central Asia 1 : 1 750 000
China - *Northeastern* 1 : 1 500 000
China - *Northern* 1 : 1 500 000
China - *Central* 1 : 1 500 000
China - *Southern* 1 : 1 500 000
Colombia - Ecuador 1 : 2 500 000
Crete - Kreta 1 : 200 000
Dominican Republic - Haiti 1 : 600 000
Egypt 1 : 2 500 000 / 1 : 750 000
Hawaiian Islands 1 : 330 000 / 1 : 125 000
Hawaiian Islands – **Kaua'i** 1 : 150 000 / 1 : 35 000
Hawaiian Islands – **Honolulu - O'ahu** 1 : 35 000 / 1 : 150 000
Hawaiian Islands – **Maui - Moloka'i - Lāna'i** 1 : 150 000 / 1 : 35 000
Hawaiian Islands – **Hawai'i, The Big Island** 1 : 330 000 / 1 : 125 000
Himalaya 1 : 1 500 000
Hong Kong 1 : 22 500
Indian Subcontinent 1 : 4 000 000
India - *Northern* 1 : 1 500 000
India - *Western* 1 : 1 500 000
India - *Eastern* 1 : 1 500 000
India - *Southern* 1 : 1 500 000
India - *Northeastern - Bangladesh* 1 : 1 500 000
Indonesia 1 : 4 000 000
Indonesia **Sumatra** 1 : 1 500 000
Indonesia **Java - Nusa Tenggara** 1 : 1 500 000
Indonesia **Bali - Lombok** 1 : 180 000
Indonesia **Kalimantan** 1 : 1 500 000
Indonesia **Java - Bali** 1 : 650 000
Indonesia **Sulawesi** 1 : 1 500 000
Indonesia **Irian Jaya - Maluku** 1 : 1 500 000
Jakarta 1 : 22 500
Japan 1 : 1 500 000
Kenya 1 : 1 100 000
Korea 1 : 1 500 000
Malaysia 1 : 1 500 000
West Malaysia 1 : 650 000
Manila 1 : 17 500
Mexico 1 : 2 500 000
Myanmar (Burma) 1 : 1 500 000
Nepal 1 : 500 000 / 1 : 1 500 000
Nepal Trekking **Khumbu Himal - Solu Khumbu** 1 : 75 000
New Zealand 1 : 1 250 000
Pakistan 1 : 1 500 000
Peru - Ecuador 1 : 2 500 000
Philippines 1 : 1 500 000
Singapore 1 : 22 500
Southeast Asia 1 : 4 000 000
South Pacific Islands 1 : 13 000 000
Sri Lanka 1 : 450 000
Taiwan 1 : 400 000
Tanzania - Rwanda, Burundi 1 : 1 500 000
Thailand 1 : 1 500 000
Uganda 1 : 700 000
Venezuela - Guyana, Suriname, French Guiana 1 : 2 500 000
Vietnam, Laos, Cambodia 1 : 1 500 000

FORTHCOMING

Bolivia, Paraguay 1 : 2 500 000
Chile 1 : 2 500 000
Cuba 1 : 775 000

Nelles Maps are top quality cartography!
Relief mapping, kilometer charts and tourist attractions.
Always up-to-date!